The
$100,000+
CAREER

The
$100,000+
CAREER

THE POWER OF
NETWORKING
FOR EXECUTIVE
JOB CHANGE

JOHN DAVIES

SOURCEBOOKS, INC.®
NAPERVILLE, ILLINOIS

Published by Sourcebooks, Inc.
P.O. Box 4410, Naperville, Illinois 60567-4410
(630) 961-3900
Fax: (630) 961-2168
www.sourcebooks.com

Library of Congress Cataloging-in-Publication Data

Davies, John
   The $100,000+ career : the power of networking for executive job
change / John Davies.
       p. cm.
   Includes index.
   ISBN-13: 978-1-4022-0654-2
   ISBN-10: 1-4022-0654-2
 1. Career changes--United States. 2. Executives--Employment--United
States. 3. Business networks--United States. 4. Social
networks--United States. 5. Job hunting--United States. I. Title: One
thousand dollar plus career. II. Title: Power of networking for executive
job change. III. Title.
   HF5384.D38 2006
   658.4'09--dc22
                                    2005033344

Printed and bound in the United States of America.
LB 10 9 8 7 6 5 4 3 2 1

For my wife, Tram, who makes my
life wonderful every day.

For my sons, Evan and Wesley, to
help them build a great network of
friends throughout their lives.

For my mom, Nancy Janet
McKenzie Davies, who helped
her kids through everything.

CONTENTS

The Power of Introduction-Based Networking • Meeting
New People • Start with Trust, Build a Network for Life

How I Developed the Law of 100 • Figuring Out What
Networking Really Means • The Art of the Introduction •
The Basics of Introduction-Based Networking

He Only Got That Job Because He Knew Her • The
Job/Contact Matrix • Service Providers and the Vendor
Network • Your Friendly Executive Recruiters • Farming
Your Past Work Life • The Power of Alumni Associations

Stanley Milgram and the Six Degrees of Separation • Strong
and Weak Ties in a Network • The Strength of Weak Ties •
Networking (Re-) Defined • From Contact to Relationship:
The Five Levels of Networking

PREFACE

NEVER BEFORE HAS RAPID change created such uncertainty in the American business landscape. The next few years will see an unprecedented rate of outsourcing, off-shoring, mergers and acquisitions, and the end to long-term employment guarantees.

According to Challenger, Gray & Christmas, some industries (such as telecommunications and high tech) will be hit significantly harder than others. If you've been sitting back thinking, "I'm entitled to a job," you'll find that there's no such thing as a guaranteed job. There's just no job with your name on it.

While this will be difficult for factory workers, those in call centers, and other labor-intensive industries, it can have a profound effect on senior executives as well if you're not prepared. To get an idea of the future world of work, new books by Tom Friedman, Roger McNamee, and Thomas Malone provide a sane perspective on the impact of global economic trends. In terms of globalization, *Los Angeles Times* business reporter James Flanigan notes the following.

> We've been here before. In the 1960s, the anxiety was over computers idling millions of workers. In the 1980s, the rise of Japanese industry was supposed to turn Americans into hamburger flippers. The nightmare visions didn't come true then, and they certainly won't come true today.
>
> Computers unleashed a huge new information industry, creating many thousands of jobs. And the competition from Japan pushed America into new frontiers such as technology and health care, where the U.S. now dominates.
>
> Likewise, globalization is creating wealth for American companies and new jobs at home as well as overseas.

However, in major economic transformations such as the rise of globalization, some U.S. workers will invariably be displaced. The types of jobs executives will be asked to oversee, manage, and perform will in many ways be different than they are today.

But these changes in the business landscape, which Sony's chairman Nobuyuki Idei compares to "the meteor that hit the Earth and killed all the dinosaurs," shouldn't be feared. There's good news for those willing to manage their careers proactively and keep an open mind.

To succeed in this new environment, you must have a strategy and framework to turn uncertain times into personal prosperity. I call this strategy "the Law of 100." It provides a practical approach that will help you flip the odds to your favor and reap the benefits of unprecedented personal and professional growth.

The Law of 100 is one part savvy advice for people new to networking, one part instructional guide for the job search process, one part personal discovery, and 100 percent critical to managing your life and career in the twenty-first century.

As executives, we must embrace the midlife reevaluation of our careers. We want more than a paycheck and have higher expectations for a more meaningful and rewarding career—we want to make a difference. While the tentative nature of job insecurity may cause some fear and uncertainty, most executives want to reclaim the enthusiasm they once had for getting up in the morning and going to work.

Whether you're currently employed or in transition, the Law of 100 can help. According to AARP, two-thirds of job seekers find jobs through networking. The problem for many, however, has been that there haven't been any books that provided a focused approach to networking for success.

The Law of 100 is here to help you follow the advice of Peter Drucker and learn that "the best way to predict the future is to create it."

INTRODUCTION

"Hi, my name is Bill. Can I help you?"
"And what makes you think I want to
know your name? I came here to eat,
not make friends! Just give me eggs
and bacon, and hold the biography!"

—*Crackpot*, by John Waters

The Power of Introduction-Based Networking

For the longest time, I didn't understand networking. At least, I didn't understand how networking really works. In my mind, I called you or had lunch with you because we had something specific to discuss. There was business to be done.

A lot of this probably came from the fact that I grew up in a town of two thousand people where you knew everyone. Getting together with people wasn't called networking, it was called living in a small town.

But when I found myself out of a job and having trouble finding the next one, I wasn't living in that small town where I knew everyone. The outplacement firm I was working with showed me the statistics—over 70 percent of jobs come through networking. From an academic perspective, I knew I had to network. I just didn't have any idea what that really meant.

The book you're holding is a practical guide to help you use networking to find the job you want. In fact, I guarantee that if you are qualified to hold your dream job, you can get it if you follow the Law of 100.

On the surface, the Law of 100 is simple. Once you have a general idea of what you want to do, you need to be *introduced* to one hundred new people. Before you reach that goal, you will have the job that you really want. It really is that simple. This book is about how you go about doing it.

First, you have to have some idea of what you want. If you haven't read *What Color Is Your Parachute?* by Richard Nelson Bolles, put this book down and go read it. Every page of Mr. Bolles's book is helpful, not just for looking for a new job, but for making sure you're finding the right job and building a better career.

Reading one book is not always enough, though. The first time I used the Law of 100, I thought I found what I wanted—I became the president of a small software company. But within a couple of months, I was more depressed than when I didn't have a job. For me, the Law of 100 worked too well, because I was using it to look for the wrong thing. But once you understand what you're looking for, you can start putting the power of the Law of 100 to work.

Meeting New People

After you figure out what you think you want to do, you need to meet new people who can help you get that job. Why? Because the people you already know would have hired you or found you a job if they could and you wouldn't be reading this book. The problem for me, once I left the friendly confines of the university and entered the working world, was that it was difficult to meet new people.

Trying to meet new people who are willing to help reminds me of the winter I left graduate school to live in Vermont. I worked as a night watchman at a ski resort, reading novels and epic poetry in preparation for my master's exam. Every Sunday morning when I got off work I would walk downtown to the newsstand and ask if I could please have a copy of the *New York Times*.

"Nope," the clerk would reply.

"But there are four of them on the shelf right behind you," I tried to politely point out.

"They're reserved."

"Can I reserve one for next week?" I asked.

"Nope," the clerk said matter-of-factly.

"Why?" I asked, not trying to be belligerent.

"We only get four copies and they're each reserved." I felt like the straight man in a Down East comedy routine. One day, after several months of repeating this ritual, a fifth copy of the Sunday *New York Times* appeared, unclaimed and mine if I wanted it. The clerk asked me if I would like it next week as well. I told him that if it wasn't too much trouble, I would really appreciate that. Only four months and I was in!

Start with Trust, Build a Network for Life

Is it really that hard to meet new people? It can be. And that brings me to my next point about the Law of 100. You need to build and nurture your relationships on a foundation of mutual trust. Obviously, the clerk in Vermont needed to know I wasn't just a temporary resident. He wanted to know that I was going to become a member of the community. For him, the investment in this relationship was not ephemeral—I would become a member of his community. Networking works in the same way—only you're building your community.

Some people like to live in small towns, and some people like to live in cities. But if you're looking for the next great job, you're going to need to leave your small town network (everyone you already know) and take a trip to the big city. You'll be surprised by how many great new people you'll meet—people who will become lifelong friends.

To give you a sense of this, during the time I wrote this book I became good friends with the consummate "car guy." For me, the most exciting car purchase was when I switched from a light truck to a sedan because I now had a dry place for golf clubs. For Charlie Hughes, a car is a branding statement—the first sentence in an individual's conversation with the rest of society.

Back in 1985 in Southern California, I was starting up a software company with a stack of credit cards and some angel money and Charlie was launching Land Rover in America. At that moment in time, I couldn't have imagined two more different people who just happened to be living in the same town. But when we were both in transition and our paths crossed, Charlie said something to me that people are often not open enough to appreciate.

"John," Charlie told me, "when most people are in transition, they're worried about their next job. But if you can find a way to relax just a little bit, you'll realize that you'll meet some of the nicest people you'll ever meet when you're in transition. When we're working, we don't have the luxury of making new acquaintances and friends outside our profession." Charlie's lesson is important because being in transition allows you to add diversity to your network, which makes it stronger and more far-reaching (an important part of building your lifelong network).

Along the way, you'll also meet people who just don't understand how all this works. After living in Vermont (and regularly enjoying the Sunday *New York Times*), I moved to San Francisco in the early eighties. One of the first meals I had in the city was at a fancy Michelin-rated restaurant. Midway through dinner, a woman at the next table slid her chair back, tapped me on the shoulder, and asked me what I was eating.

"Excuse me?" I said.

"Is that the veal?" she asked, and then stood up and walked over to one of my companions and said, "Oh, that fish looks delicious." I remember at that moment thinking that everything I'd been told about the West Coast was probably true.

Before I started using the Law of 100, I felt the same way about networking as I felt about that woman. She was boorish and certainly not making any new friends. Why would I want to introduce myself to complete strangers? Especially if what I was doing was trying to find a job.

Being a generally stubborn individual, it took me a while to realize that when it is done correctly, networking is the only "controllable" way you can get a new job. And not just a job, but something that you really want to do, an advancement in your career.

Once you know what you want, then you can use the Law of 100 to find it. I did it twice for employment in one year, and as I maintain my network I continue to use the same principles outlined in this book. Through my speaking and writing, I have helped people ranging from high school graduates to CEOs discover that the Law of 100 really works.

But the best thing I found out was that by using this approach and building a bigger community, I started living a fuller life. Not that I didn't enjoy the small-town life of my friends and family before. It's just that now I have a lot more friends who can help me not only find the next great thing to do, but who I can also share these experiences with.

CHAPTER 1

THE LAW OF 100

"You know nothing of me. Surely you ought not to recommend a person who is a stranger to you?"

—*The Two Destinies*, by Wilkie Collins

How I Developed the Law of 100

I didn't really want to write a book about looking for a job. I was employed and making what most people would consider a lot of money. As cofounder of a software company eighteen years before, I had built a growing and profitable business. But twelve years after bootstrapping a start-up, my business partner and I thought there was a quicker path to fortune.

As the first step toward going public, we raised over $10 million in venture capital. As part of the deal, we started recruiting the "professional" management team the investors wanted to see in place.

Wisely, my cofounder cashed out. I kept my investment and stayed in the background with the dream that this team would create my retirement fund.

For the next few years, the company lost money at a staggering rate. After reinserting myself into the business, my discussions with the CEO I had recruited became more confrontational. I ignored him for a while and worked closely with the COO to get the company back to breaking even. But the disagreements between me and the CEO only got worse, as we had very different views about the business. One day while playing golf, we formally agreed to disagree. That's a polite way to put it and if the roles were reversed, I would have fired me before we ever got to the back nine. But we agreed it was "just business, nothing personal." Maybe that's what bothered me—I couldn't understand anyone who didn't take the company's performance personally.

I went home that night and faced the unpleasant realization that my job had lost its purpose. I didn't want to explain to my young children that I was sleepwalking through a job I no longer cared about and that was no longer fun. I didn't want to explain more layoffs to long-time employees. I decided to leave, with an optimistic outlook toward the future.

I took the holidays off and played with my kids. I took long walks every morning and was back to see them before they went to school. I went to conferences on nanotechnology and read novels I had always wanted to read. After the New Year, it was time to find a job. I wanted the next job along the trajectory of my career—CEO of a software company in Southern California. I worked on my resume and marketing strategy at the outplacement firm. I read *Rites of Passage* to find out about how executive search firms worked. I was on my way.

I began my search with the blind confidence that this couldn't be more difficult than starting a new company. But after a few months, I wasn't getting interviews. And what I was learning wasn't making me feel optimistic any more.

One spring morning, I was talking with Peter Sobiloff, a managing director at Insight Venture Capital. I wanted to know how many CEOs were hired within their portfolio of companies. Out of forty companies, they had placed one (who happened to be a friend of mine and who I knew was a better fit for that company than I ever could have been). Furthermore, Peter said, they weren't really placing many executive positions because "if the management teams made it through the last couple of years of cost containment, we're going to give them a chance to show they can now grow a business." My spider sense should have been tingling.

A few days later I was in Santa Monica at another venture capital firm. I met with one of their venture partners who had been brought on to evaluate "human capital." He told me that they hadn't changed a CEO in one of their portfolio companies for at least a year, but "Let's just pretend there's an opening and I've got a stack of three hundred resumes on my desk."

He went down the list of the selection criteria they would use in evaluating me against the other candidates. First, I had never had the title before and there were lots of previously successful CEOs in transition who had taken a couple of companies public or done some major mergers and acquisitions work. Then there was another set of CEOs who had the same pedigree but were unhappy at their current company. After that came the CEOs who were currently happy but could be lured with money and stock.

Next on the list came vice presidents and general managers from SAP or Oracle, and then lesser software firms. Perhaps they would look at senior partners at one of the large consulting organizations such as Accenture or IBM. There were also venture capitalists who wanted to be CEOs…the list continued to grow.

"And," he went on, "when I read your resume I see you've done a little bit of everything—directing sales, marketing, development, product management, services, even support. Companies aren't just hiring a general management suit. They're looking for a forty-one-long, double-breasted, dark-gray pinstripe with one-inch cuffs. And even when they're that specific, there's still a rack to choose from. When I look at that stack of 300 resumes, you're around number 287!" I may have been wearing Armani, but I felt like Leisure Suit Larry.

At that point, the managing director joined us, and we continued talking. "John," he said enthusiastically, "I really like you. You've accomplished some really great things. But do you know why you're not having any luck finding a leadership role in a software company in Southern California?" We were sitting in an office in Santa Monica, the sun glistening on the ocean. I sat up a little straighter, ready for the veil to be drawn aside. In response, I would once again point out all that I had accomplished. I would answer objections by following all the correct interviewing techniques I had learned from the outplacement firm.

"The reason you can't find that job is that there *are* no software companies in Southern California!"

'Outrageous, I thought, until we tried to name more than ten good-sized software companies in Southern California. While there were definitely more than ten, the point was there weren't dozens, much less hundreds. My initial reaction now changed to an emotion that could be characterized by one simple word—"Oops."

Over the course of my search, I met numerous VCs and private equity managers who were looking to invest in Southern California and couldn't find a place to put their money. Most of them would ask me, "Why don't you start something?" and I'd always reply that "I haven't found a good problem to solve." Secretly I thought, "I've got a wife, two young kids, and need to start making money before the end of the year."

I needed to change my tactics. As I drove back home and replayed that meeting in my mind, I kept thinking about the imaginary stack of resumes sitting on the human capital manager's desk. I could no longer visualize a board member or a company founder picking up their job specification and my resume and shouting "Eureka! We've found a match!" I could have John Grisham write my resume and it would still be difficult to state my case on paper. There would have to be some other way for me to get past the other 286 applicants.

The next day I went to have a cup of coffee with Richard Guha, a man who had been a corporate officer in three major corporations as well as a CEO, CMO, and board member of several companies. I had met Rich at a biweekly meeting of technology executives "in transition" where he stood out because:

a) He wasn't "in transition" in terms of career, but more in terms of geography,

b) He had a great British accent, and

c) He had just finished writing a book.

It took several attempts, but we finally got together to discuss my search and his migration to Southern California. After I relayed my recent findings to Rich, he told me that 30 percent of senior executives in Silicon Valley were unemployed (an executive recruiter later told me, "That's probably a conservative estimate").

I knew I should have been more depressed, but I felt liberated. "I" wasn't the only thing preventing me from finding a job if there wasn't a job to find. That meant my search would have to broaden.

Figuring Out What Networking Really Means

I hadn't used job boards because I don't believe anyone truthfully advertises for a CEO. I will confess, though, that I've had lunch with the CFO of a successful software company who found his job through Monster.com. Even after meeting him and hearing that story, I still didn't think job boards were the best place for an executive to search.

I knew from numerous studies that approximately 15 percent of people get hired through responding to ads or job boards and 15 percent get placed by recruiters. That leaves the other 70 percent, of which I was clearly a member. This was the promised land of networking and informational interviews, and the hidden job market.

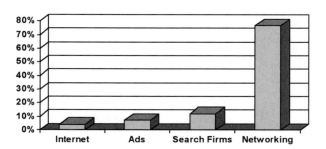

But how was I supposed to go from not working to networking? I sat down for lunch with Casper "Cap" Zublin to talk about what I had been doing lately. This was the second time I was having lunch with Cap since being introduced by a mutual friend. But the real way I got to this point ends up looking like assembly directions to a Rube Goldberg machine.

1. Outplacement firm hosts monthly meeting for senior executives "in transition."

2. One guy, let's call him Michael Wakeman (because that's what his parents called him), has an interesting background and he thinks I do too. We talk and exchange business cards (yes, you still need a business card when you're looking for a job, but more about what kind of business card in chapter 4).

3. Michael sends me an email with some tips for my search. I later realize that the big takeaway here is that even though Michael was trying to land his next gig as a chief marketing officer, he connected with me first by trying to offer some help.

4. I call Michael and we agree to meet for a cup of coffee. We talk about each other's background, what we're looking for, how our

search has been going. Michael suggests a couple people I might be interested in meeting—Cal and Cap (trust me, these are their real names).

5. I have lunch with Cal. While he's a nice enough guy, there's little we connect on. He's taken an interim position running a friend's business and has found he really enjoys not having to travel constantly and the extra time he gets to spend with his family. But he has no idea how to help me.

6. I play phone and email tag with Cap's assistant until we finally set up a time to have lunch.

7. We have lunch and end up having a great conversation about our work, our families, where we've lived. Cap makes a note to email a couple of people as an introduction to me.

8. A month goes by, and neither of the people has contacted me, so I set up another lunch with Cap. This time, right after lunch, he sends emails to them and copies me—he does this right while I'm sitting in his office.

Why am I telling you this? Because these eight steps illustrate the power and the process of networking. One person leads to another. And while not everyone can help you, the Law of 100 will give you a structured way to rapidly expand your network and increase your networking success.

But first, let's get back to my lunch with Cap. If it sounds like it took a long time to get there, you're right. As described later in the book, you need to reach a level of trust with people before they can really help you. Once we established that trust, Cap was more willing to help me. In fact, here's the story Cap told me that afternoon that gave me the idea for the Law of 100.

Casper Zublin graduated from business school with his MBA, and with his girlfriend halfway across the country. As he was just getting out of school, he didn't have a lot to move, so he packed everything into his car and moved to be with his girlfriend.

He'd already received an offer letter from a large consulting firm and all he had to do was dot the i's and cross the t's. What Cap didn't know was that there was a change in upper management, and that the partner who had hired him was no longer with the firm. When he walked in that Monday, the formality of signing an offer letter turned into a formal interview.

He botched it. When he walked into the office that morning, he wasn't ready to be grilled by the firm's new managing partner and they clearly didn't hit it off. Cap left their offices dejected. He had no prospects back at his alma mater and he wanted to stay with his girlfriend.

Cap started thinking about his options. He knew he could be successful as a consultant if he could just get a chance to prove himself. He knew it would take too long if he tried to advertise his services in a newspaper. And he knew that the traditional forms of direct marketing—sending letters to every business in the area—would take too long to sit around and wait for a reply.

But then he started thinking about the "metrics" associated with direct marketing, and the light bulb went off in his head. He remembered from his marketing classes that direct mailing usually produced a response between 1 percent to 3 percent. "That might not seem like much for all the effort," he thought, "but I only need one job right now. If I just call the top one hundred companies in the area, I should be able to get some consulting work."

He started calling the top one hundred local businesspeople. At first, he talked about his wide range of skills and abilities. But he soon realized that the more specific he was in describing the particular expertise he had to offer, the more people could help him find someone who could use his services. If the person he met didn't want to hire him, they usually knew someone else he might want to talk with.

Each time he met someone, he told them what number they were. By the time he met the eighty-seventh person, he was hired to help a business work on their strategic planning. He loved the job and the work he did with them led to other opportunities—his career was on its way.

Later that day, I started thinking about Cap's story. His approach was a classic selling strategy—"If you make one hundred cold calls, one person will buy." I tried to think about how that would apply to my search. There certainly weren't one hundred small software companies easily found outside of Silicon Valley, and it didn't seem possible that simply meeting one hundred people from a range of local software companies was the right criteria.

The Art of the Introduction

At a number of organized networking meetings, I would sometimes meet thirty or more people at a lunch or dinner. We all congregated at a common location with a common goal (this thing called networking), but that's where the bond ended. Meeting one hundred people this way was like fishing with dynamite.

While I have nothing against occasionally fishing with dynamite, I felt that this wasn't a great way to meet new people who could help me (although it is a great way to keep in touch with people you already know). But the foundation of the idea—applying some metrics to my networking efforts—made a lot of sense.

I started to think about how I could still keep the target at one hundred but define the criteria in a way that I reached my goal of finding a really great job. Through trial and error (and a lot of phone calls), I decided that the way to fine-tune the approach was not just to meet new people (because that is too easy and too random), but to be *introduced* to new people.

The idea of an introduction, or the more formal letter of introduction, is a powerful concept dating back thousands of years. Whether it is Pythagoras's visit to Egypt with a letter of introduction written by Polycrates or the letter John Smith wrote to Queen Anne regarding Pocahontas's visit to England, a formal introduction has cleared the way for many travelers.

Before the Internet and the telephone, the common business practice was a formal letter of introduction. In the nineteenth century, no one would consider seeking new employment in a town or city unless they carried with them a letter of introduction from a friend or associate who was willing to vouch for the character and qualifications of the individual.

In *The Art of Letter Writing* (anonymously published in 1907), the author notes that: "Letters of introduction are one of the common methods of establishing social relations. The person who is not known to your friend can become known through your kind offices. In this way, very often, important services can be rendered."

While the tone is slightly archaic, the advice is still sound for any type of introduction, as exhibited by the following passage. "Never give a letter of introduction unless you thoroughly understand the character and manners of the person to whom you write the letter and also of the person whom the letter introduces.

"You have no right, to avoid giving offence or through sheer inability to say no to a request, to foist upon your distant friend someone whose acquaintance he will not thank you for and who may prove a very undesirable visitor. If one or the other of the two parties concerned must be offended, let it be the applicant. You can usually give some sufficient reason for declining—but decline in any event if the person is likely to prove objectionable."

The art of the introduction, whether it's by letter, email, telephone, or in person, is simple. The effect, however, is extremely powerful. An introduction provides immediate legitimacy. A personal introduction means that the person acting as the intermediary trusts you enough to introduce you to someone they know and also trust.

The Basics of Introduction-Based Networking

The Law of 100. It sounds simple and it is. Once you know your goal (what you define as your next great job), you need to be introduced to one hundred new people. The following chapters provide you with a step-by-step game plan for using the Law of 100 in your job search. But before we get into the details, let me tell you the rest of the story of my search as I developed the Law of 100 approach and the tools that go with it.

Before I figured out the Law of 100, I traveled down dead-ends for four months. I revised my resume numerous times, I looked online for job postings, and I continued to try to meet executive recruiters. At the same time I was doing all of those things that didn't really help me, I was also learning about networking. Specifically, I was learning about introduction-based networking. I started following the organized networking plan laid out in the book you're holding. And I started to have success.

After two months of using the Law of 100 approach, I found eight opportunities to pursue. Two were complete garbage. Two were in a different city, but the companies looked interesting (even though they weren't immediate opportunities to be a CEO). I consulted at both companies briefly and got paid to find out I didn't want to work there or move to San Jose.

One day I got a phone call from someone I hadn't even been introduced to. He asked for my resume since he was doing a board search for the president of a company. And there was at least one executive search for a chief marketing officer that got put on hold until the CEO could have lunch with me and gauge my interest.

I also reconnected with a company founder who'd been following my career and wanted to hire me to lead a small software company twenty miles away from my home. I hit the jackpot and got my personal validation that the Law of 100 worked.

It was then that I discovered that the Law of 100 can work too well. After two months on the job, I wasn't happy. The company was undercapitalized and trying to compete in an overcrowded market. The job I thought I wanted and the job I got did not line up. The CEO's job in a small company is over 99 percent operational and tactical, and at this point in my life I needed something that utilized my creative talents. I managed a graceful exit—leaving the business slightly better than when I joined.

I was back on the street once again, and now the "family to feed" clock was ticking louder. I turned to the Law of 100 once more—only this time with a twist. By applying some of the same metrics and methodologies, I called on my network to help me figure out what my next move (and career) should be. I chose a wide range of people to help me—a mix of personal friends, family, former coworkers, vendors, clients, as well as new friends I had met during my networking activities. I confessed to each of them that I had been looking for the wrong job. About half of them replied, "We didn't think you'd be happy as a CEO, but you were so determined that we didn't feel it was our place to change your mind."

I further confided that my singular focus on becoming a CEO had prevented me from exploring other opportunities. I needed to change direction and I needed some answers fast. I asked each of them two questions. If you were my personal agent:

+ What role would you pitch me for?
+ What types of organizations would you then call on?

Astonishingly, the feedback I got was positive and consistent. Most of the people I talked with had insightful advice and a good perspective in terms of what I should be doing. No one in my network identified a specific job opportunity, but each of them described the same attributes that would make me happy. I needed something that allowed for my creativity, a role that balanced "doing" with "leading others." They gave me ideas as to the types of titles and companies I might be looking for.

And they gave me more introductions. The door was opened once again, only this time the transition moved much faster because I was looking for a job that existed rather than trying to find the proverbial needle in a haystack. Within a month I was having discussions with three firms and was soon hired as vice president of strategy for AMR Research.

The Law of 100 works. At one level, this book is a fun and practical guide to teach job seekers how to use networking to find the job they want. The primary focus—a technique called "introduction-based networking"—will bring success to anyone. The Law of 100 is unique in that it:

1. Describes how networking can be specifically used to help the job seeker,
2. Provides a set of techniques and tools that can be immediately applied for a more effective and efficient job search, and
3. Creates a fun approach to the search process that makes it dynamic and rewarding.

It's all about people. People will help you get your new job. As the later chapters illustrate, the Law of 100 is about more than just a job search technique. It's a way of creating a larger network that can help you during good times as well as times of need. It provides a strategy for staying current in your career while positioning yourself for greater opportunities. The lessons learned here can be applied throughout your career to create your own managed job security.

So now that you know what the Law of 100 is, it's time to learn how to use it. The next chapter will help you figure out who you've met in the past and how they can help you with introductions in the future.

> The Law of 100
> is
> *Introduction-Based Networking*

It is a strategy specifically developed to help executives transition to the job they want. The Law of 100 is based on the following principles:

It's Not Just What You Know—your past knowledge and accomplishments only help when people are looking for you (in which case you're probably employed) or you've found who you want to talk with (and now you're selling the vision of you working there).

It's Not Just Who You Know—personal networks tend to be insular, meaning that you know most of the people your friends know and they all know about the same opportunities.

It's Who They Know—by reaching beyond your close friends, by connecting with "weaker" networking links, you will find a much greater number of opportunities that you never would have known about. You will find the job you want!

CHAPTER 2

IT'S NOT WHAT YOU KNOW, IT'S WHO YOU KNOW

*"It is not so much our friends' **help** that helps us as the confident knowledge that they **will** help us."*

—Epicurus

SINCE THE LAW OF 100 is all about introduction-based networking, you need to think about the people who can make those introductions. To help you figure out who you know, the following chapter provides you with the first of the Law of 100 tools—the job/contact matrix. Once you identify all your former coworkers and current friends in the matrix, you can start talking with them about who they know and who they can introduce to you.

When I first started coming up with the idea for this book, I was introduced to Terry Goldfarb-Lee, a woman whose enthusiasm and spirit are contagious.

Terry publishes the *Directory of Orange County [California] Networking Organizations* to help people connect more easily. The following chapter is my attempt to capture the "Terry Goldfarb-Lee Experience." I may not be able to recreate her enthusiasm and energy, but what she has to share is important to your path toward leveraging the Law of 100.

He Only Got That Job Because He Knew Her

There is a very high probability that this won't be the last time you are looking for a job. In fact, on average people change jobs every two and a half years. Unfortunately, for many the change is not by choice. For that reason, you need to prepare thoroughly now. In other words, you need to start building the foundation for your networking activities and, most important, keep the process alive.

During my transition, it was not uncommon to run across a story such as this one paraphrased from the Dow Jones "Venture Wire" e-newsletter.

"Company X announced it has a new chief executive, its fourth in about three years. The new CEO is David, who once headed a now-scaled-down firm selling products online. Most recently, he worked as a venture capital advisor. David succeeds Tom, who served as acting president from September until about this month. Previously, Dick had been interim CEO until roughly July 2003 and, before him, Harry had filled the post. Tom, Dick, and Harry couldn't be reached for comment."

The only thing missing from this story is the ubiquitous explanation that Tom left "to pursue other interests." In TheStreet.com's "The Five Dumbest Things on Wall Street This Week," George Mannes once observed that he would enjoy it if, as a possible off-shoot of Sarbanes-Oxley, "Companies were required to supply real-world, non-euphemistic reasons as to why executives were departing from their companies.... Imagine one day reading that Executive X resigned from the Company because 'the CEO had grown to loathe him.'"

And how many times have you seen situations where you think to yourself, "Blank it, the only reason Sam got that job is because he knew Lucinda, the hiring manager."

Now step back and put yourself in Lucinda's place—given a slate of candidates with relatively equal qualifications, the tie-breaker goes to someone you can trust. And trustworthiness, as well as the vagaries of bosses and venture capitalists, doesn't show up very well on a resume.

The Job/Contact Matrix

It all boils down to the fact that people are more likely to help people they know. The problem for most people is how do you figure out who you know? And the common surprise is—you know a lot more people than you think you do.

One of the best tools for this is what Terry Goldfarb-Lee calls the "Job/Contact Matrix." Here is an example of the Job/Contact Matrix.

Job/Contact Matrix

Company	CPA Firm	Bankers	Attorneys	Investment Bankers	Fin'l Printers	Leasing	Real Estate	Direct Reports	Reported to	Others in company	Insura
ABC	Joe Smith-		Joe Small-								
Company	Partner	Al Good-	Sr. Ptnr	Sam Green							
	Jean Brown-		Bill Murray-								
	Mgr		Jr. Prt								
DEF Company											
GHI Company											
College Alumni	**People I know**	**Company I am targeting**									
Undergraduate											
Graduate School											
Company Alumni	**People I know**	**Company I am targeting**									
Big 4											
Major company											

The easiest way to build this matrix is to use a spreadsheet and fill in the blanks. Across the top row of the matrix, you list categories of the types of vendors and service providers you've worked with over the course of your career. For example, if you're looking to become the VP of Finance or the CFO, the top line of your matrix might include the following:

+ CPA firms
+ Bankers
+ Attorneys
+ Investment bankers
+ Financial printers
+ Leasing companies
+ Real estate companies/brokers

If you're not in finance, you need to pull out your resume and look at each accomplishment you've listed and think about who you worked with to achieve that success. If you're in manufacturing, don't just think about the material suppliers but include the maintenance and repair companies right next to the toolmakers.

Service Providers and the Vendor Network

Building out this top line of the matrix with service providers and vendors is important for a very simple, and mostly overlooked, reason.

> Service providers and the vendor network are the number one competition to retained search firms.
>
> They know where the jobs are.

A large number of jobs get placed via this network, jobs that never reach the search firms. Why is this network of service providers and suppliers so powerful? The answer is twofold and can be summed up in the following equation:

$$\text{Trust} + \text{Access} = \text{Influence}$$

The first part of the equation, "trust," should be obvious. These individuals wouldn't be working with their clients if they hadn't performed well and earned their trust as an advisor.

The "access" part of the equation is equally critical. As Woody Allen once observed, "Ninety percent of life is just showing up." This network of providers shows up on a regular basis. They have access to the water cooler. While walking around their client's company, they could easily be mistaken for an employee.

I remember a sales rep named Bob Wolkowitz who used to stop by our offices every Friday afternoon. His much larger competitor had a seat on our board of directors and was a clear category leader in the minds of our customers. But a few of our customers used Bob's equipment, and so every Friday afternoon Bob would stop by to see how we were doing. Occasionally he would ring my office from the lobby to see if I had five minutes free, but mostly he would just check in with our engineers to see if there was anything they needed.

Soon, Bob became a fixture at our company. He knew all our sales reps and many of our engineers. Nothing externally changed in our business, but Bob's share of our spending increased. He eventually sold as much equipment to us as his competitor for the simple reason that he was always available and had earned our trust.

Any company's service provider network is filled with individuals like Bob. And it's not because they're constantly selling—rather because they're constantly making sure they're providing good service to their customers. As a result, they become trusted partners. Partners, by the way, who can recommend people for a job.

Your Friendly Executive Recruiters

While service providers may represent the biggest competition to executive search firms, you shouldn't ignore the executive search firms you've used to hire subordinates or who have tried to recruit you. This is your chance to get something back from them. It's unreasonable to think that you'll have the luck of perfect timing for the searches they are currently working on. But the untapped potential of most professional recruiters lies in the networks they participate in and maintain. These are networks of contacts who are out there ready to help you if you could just connect (and getting those meetings is what the rest of this book is about).

But before leaving the topic of executive recruiters, there are a few basic tips and approaches that can be helpful when discussing your job search with them. First, there are basically two kinds of recruiters, those who work on a contingency basis and those who are retained.

As an executive, there is almost no advantage in talking with a contingency-based recruiter and, even worse, there is a lot of risk in sending him or her your resume. The contingency recruiter gets paid only when someone they submit to a company gets hired. This results in a "mass market" set of activities by the recruiter. Immediately upon receiving your resume, it is their goal to get it into as many hands and as many companies as possible—before someone else does. This will result in their being credited for introducing you to your next prospective employer.

Now put yourself behind the employer's desk. Your resume arrives unsolicited and untargeted—blind to whether there is any role for you at the company or not. It's the equivalent of trying to meet your future bride by walking around a grocery store and asking each woman you meet whether she would marry you.

If you believe that the only reason you're not getting offers is because the companies have somehow misplaced your resume, skip the contingency search firms, get a business directory, and start mailing (and when you get back to planet Earth, send me an email).

It's a completely different ballgame though when it comes to retained search. The retained search firms are paid whether their client hires any of the candidates the firm presents or not. Obviously, the retained firm requires a good track record of placing candidates for a client or the client won't retain them for the next search.

When you're in transition, remember that "the damned headhunter" (the retained search executive) is being paid by his client and not by you. That client is not a charitable organization dedicated to helping you out. They did not start their engagement by asking, "Who's on the bench right now?" They started with a very specific profile of the ideal candidate and a list of companies where the ideal candidate worked.

At any given time, an executive recruiter is personally working on a very small number of searches. This limits the chance that the moment you contact her is the same moment she's performing a search where you would be an ideal candidate. That doesn't mean you shouldn't let them know your accomplishments as you progress through your career (sort of like sending them periodic news clippings about you).

Many retained recruiters like to "discover" candidates. This means that you need to be able to be found. Throughout your career, it is wise to position yourself in the marketplace—whether it's by writing articles for industry publications or speaking at industry events. This is discussed more in the chapter on building your personal brand.

When you're in transition, though, add the retained recruiters to your matrix of contacts to get information about your industry, tips about local networking events, and introductions to people who can help you in your search. Conversations about these topics won't put a recruiter on the defensive. And they'll likely remember your initiative and look forward to the next time you meet.

Farming Your Past Work Life

Once you've listed all the vendors and service providers across the top row of the matrix, you need to add two more columns:

+ Direct Reports
+ Reported To

People you have worked for and people who have worked for you both know you very well. They know your strengths and more than likely (unless you've torched all your bridges) will be willing and eager to help you if they can.

Now that you've listed all the categories of companies or people across the top of the matrix, you need to list the companies you've worked for along the left side of the matrix. If you've been at a particular company for an extended period of time, you may want to divide this by "positions held" or "projects worked on."

Now that you've laid out the matrix, it becomes an exercise of trying to remember all the people's names that will fill in the boxes. It's not unlike trying to figure out the answer when your spouse asks, "Where do you want to go to dinner tonight?"

When people try to think of restaurants off the top of their head, they tend to focus on a very few. But if they created something similar to the Job/Contact Matrix, they would create a row of "types" of restaurants across the top (including French, Italian, Japanese, Thai, etc.). They could then list the restaurants they know under each category. The list always ends up being longer and more comprehensive when you have prompts to help you remember.

The Power of Alumni Associations

In the same way that you've listed the companies that you've worked for in order to determine service providers and others who have helped you in the past, you need to start looking for other alumni associations. The first, and most obvious, is the school (or schools) that you graduated from.

You can start by creating a similar sheet as the Job/Contact Matrix. Along the left column you can list your undergraduate and graduate schools. Depending on how good or bad the memories are, you may even choose to list your high school.

During one of my many speaking engagements that helped me develop this book, I met a woman who walked into a job interview and immediately recognized her old high school classmate. During the hour-long interview, they compared notes as to who was now doing what. Of course, as a part of that they talked about what she had done—it just didn't have the same sense of "interrogation" that she had felt at other interviews. The next day she found out she had the job.

It is probably a safe assumption that for the majority of people, their next interview isn't going to be with a former classmate. But that doesn't mean you shouldn't be getting back in touch with them.

Many universities have put copies of their alumni directories online. Others provide bound copies of their directories—particularly during years when reunions are scheduled. The online directories are more useful because of the ease of searching them, but the most important thing is to have the directory (in whatever form you can get it).

Alumni directories are helpful because while you are scanning the names of your former classmates, you occasionally remember friends you've lost touch with, and there's no better time to reconnect with them than the present.

Across the top line of your Alumni Matrix, you should have two distinct columns. The first column is where you list people you know. The second column is where you list people you want to meet who work at the companies you are targeting.

With many of the online directories, you can do keyword searches to find alumni who currently work at or have worked at the companies you are targeting. When you find someone, give him a call at his office and introduce yourself as a fellow alumnus who is interested in finding out more about his company. It's hard to resist the call of a fellow Blue Hen (or Terrapin, or Anteater, or Bruin). This same approach works well for sororities and fraternities too.

One of the truly great features of alumni groups is that alumni tend to like people who like their institution. It's a matter of school pride—you didn't have to go to school in Atlanta to be an honorary Yellow Jacket.

For example, more than twenty thousand Harvard Business School (HBS) alumni in thirty-nine countries throughout the world belong to one hundred nine HBS clubs and associations. While I didn't get an MBA from Harvard, I've benefited by attending my local club's breakfast meetings.

These meetings usually focus on topics of broad professional interest, with speakers drawn from industry, government, education, the arts, or other managerial backgrounds. In addition to presenting interesting and educational information, these breakfasts are a great opportunity for networking and socializing. And you don't have to be a Harvard graduate to attend.

During my search, I started attending Harvard Business School events. I also started attending West Point events and I'm still not sure which of these two great institutions I'm less qualified to be associated with. Living in Southern California also meant I have a lot of friends who are alumni of either UCLA or USC or Pepperdine who might look up names in their directories for me.

When researching your target companies, make sure to check the executive biographies (either on their website, in their annual reports, or just by Googling them). If they went to Harvard (or a university in your

region), you may have friends who can make an introduction "as an alumni helping out a friend."

> The power of a common bond
> can extend to you as well:
>
> "Any friend of an alumnus
> is a friend of mine."

Another set of alumni you should investigate are
"company alumni"—specifically alumni of a company you've targeted for employment. For example,
in Southern California there's a group of former
Allergan employees who refer to themselves as
Allergones. They hold yearly reunions and other
events throughout the year. If you ever wanted to be
hired at Allergan, this is the first alumni group you
should contact.

There are many other companies that have
alumni organizations, including the large consulting
firms and most major companies. To find out
whether a university or company has an alumni association in your area, you can search on the Web.
For example, in the Los Angeles area, you can check
out www.at-la.com and find all types of university
and organizational directories.

The Most Important Part of Building Your List
As a result of this exercise, you should now have a fairly substantial list of people you can contact. As you develop this list and begin talking with people, you need to remember Terry's Golden Rule:

Don't prejudge!

This is especially important for expanding your list of contacts beyond the people you went to school with or who knew you from your work. You should think about expanding your network with some of the following.
+ Neighbors
+ Barber or hair salon
+ Fledglings
+ Shopkeepers

These are all people you see regularly during the course of your day. In terms of networking, most people "prejudge"—that is, they assume their neighbor or their hair stylist can't really help. If you think that way, you're making a big mistake. For the most part, these are people who meet lots of other people every single day.

Terry told me a story once about trying to sell into a very large distributor of pharmaceutical and health care products. For years she tried everything she could to get a meeting with a senior executive and she finally got an introduction to the CFO.

After meeting with him, he walked her down the hall and told her she'd need to work with the controller.

They exchanged business cards and Terry asked him where he lived. "Irvine," he said.

"Oh," said Terry, "I live in Irvine, too."

"Well," he replied more specifically, "I live in Woodbridge."

"That's interesting," said Terry, "I live in Woodbridge too. What street do you live on?"

"Shooting Star," the controller replied.

"I live on Shooting Star, too," said Terry. It turns out that they had been neighbors for seven years! As a result of that incident, Terry decided to hold a block party every year so that all of her neighbors could meet and get to know each other better.

To emphasize her point about not prejudging people, Terry also advises people to talk to local business proprietors, such as hair stylists. Although this isn't intuitively obvious for many people, it didn't surprise me—primarily because Ryan Shuck, who cuts my hair when he's not on tour, is the guitarist in a band. Ryan is as comfortable barbecuing with Chester from Linkin Park as he is at dinner with Michael Dell. And as strange as it seemed when he told me his story of dining with Michael Dell, he was actually there as the guest of Nick, another technology company's CEO. While this dinner was a friendly get-together between two CEOs, it eventually led to Ryan working with Nick on some new business ideas.

What you should understand, though, is that while Ryan is one of the nicest people you could meet, he's decorated with tattoos, has a range of varying hair colors and styles, and doesn't dress in Brooks Brothers suits (to say the least). But when it comes to being connected to a diverse network of people, Ryan's got it in spades. And as you'll see in the next chapter, a more diverse network creates greater opportunities.

Finally, you can't forget about fledglings. Fledglings are people at work who were just starting their careers when you met. Terry once told me about Bill, the CFO of one of the world's largest manufacturing companies, who found himself in transition after the company decided to relocate its headquarters. One day Bill ran into a young man who had been a service technician in the company's IT department when Bill first came on board several years before. When he asked Bill what he was doing, Bill explained that he was in transition and looking for a new opportunity. The technician told Bill that he recently heard that they were looking for a CFO at the company he was now working at and that he could find out what the process was. Over the next week, they worked together to get Bill an introduction to the president and he was eventually hired as the company's CFO.

Keeping positive relations, even with fledglings, can often help you out in the future.

Now That You Know Who You Know

You're now on your way to a large list of people who really want to help you. Of course, you are capturing that information to start developing your database (more on that in chapter 10). But before you start making calls to all these people, you need to think about how well you know them. If you worked with someone on a daily basis, they will unquestionably introduce you to people in their network who might be able to help. But if you only saw them for a day once a year, you might think about having lunch together and letting them get to know you a little better before you start asking big favors.

In the next chapter, I discuss the five levels of networking and how to build relationships with the people in your network. By building stronger relationships, you'll not only build better friendships, you'll get introduced to the best contacts they know because you will have built a foundation of trust. So let's think once more about who you should talk with right away and then start building that foundation.

People I Should Talk with Tomorrow
Even if you're not in transition, you should put together a list of all the people you need to start talking to that you interact with on a regular basis. Most of them probably like you and would enjoy the conversation. Go talk with:

+ The auditor who knew my uncle in New Jersey.
+ The lady who cuts my hair.
+ My kid's soccer coach.
+ That guy in accounting who used to thank me for listing all my clients on my expense reports.
+ The woman who tried to recruit me to join _____ as a senior executive.

Now you can add your own people to this list:

+ _____
+ _____
+ _____
+ _____

THEORIES OF NETWORKING AND THE FIVE LEVELS OF NETWORKING SUCCESS

"The best time to make friends is before you need them."

—Ethel Barrymore

A CCORDING TO *The American Heritage Dictionary of the English Language*, one of the definitions of a network is: "An extended group of people with similar interests or concerns who interact and remain in informal contact for mutual assistance or support."

According to common sense, it's usually a good idea to avoid starting a presentation (or a chapter in a book) with a quote from the dictionary. I once watched a salesman start a presentation by defining the word business—he included all eleven entries from his dictionary and proceeded to read each one of them to us. To invert a line from the movie *Jerry Maguire*, you lost me at "commercial, industrial, or professional dealings."

But I included the formal definition for networking to stress the point that a network is "an extended group of people" and not just a collection of close friends and relatives. For networking to be truly useful in your search, you need to extend beyond the people you already know. To help in understanding the impact of the network effect, the next chapter provides a quick primer on networking theories and then quickly starts you on the path of turning theory into useful steps for building your network.

Stanley Milgram and the Six Degrees of Separation

The study of human networks is a relatively recent phenomenon. Theories about social networks view relationships in terms of *nodes* and *ties*. Nodes are the individuals within the networks and ties are the relationships between them. These can be mapped in simple diagrams such as the one here.

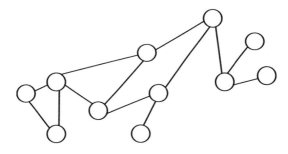

As recently as forty years ago, it was assumed that networks were somewhat random, with nodes distributed across a bell curve, dominated by averages. But the work of Stanley Milgram in 1967 presented a new way to look at social networks in terms of "degrees of separation."

Actually, the initial theory of six degrees of separation—that anyone on the planet can be connected to any other person on the planet through no more than five intermediaries—was first proposed in 1929 in a short story called "Chains" by the Hungarian writer Frigyes Karinthy. It took sociologist Stanley Milgram to revive this theory and apply a more scientific structure to test what he called the "small world problem." There are a number of variations to this experiment conducted by Milgram, but in essence he randomly recruited dozens of people in Kansas and asked them to forward a letter through their personal connections to a complete stranger in Boston, Massachusetts. The senders knew the recipient's name, occupation, and general location. They were instructed to send the letter to a person they knew on a first-name basis who they thought was most likely, out of all their friends, to know the target personally. That person would do the same, and so on, until the letter was personally delivered to its target recipient.

Although the participants expected the chain to include at least a hundred intermediaries, it only took (on average) between five and seven intermediaries to get each letter delivered. Milgram's findings were published in *Psychology Today* and inspired the phrase "six degrees of separation." This later inspired the popular game "Six Degrees of Kevin Bacon" developed by three college friends who went to Albright College (Reading, PA). Their theory was that Kevin Bacon is the center of the entertainment universe, and that any actor or actress can be linked back to him, typically within six degrees (six connections).

One of the interesting aspects of Milgram's work was that there seemed to be "Kevin Bacons" (i.e., people more well-connected than others) at work in his experiment. Milgram noticed a funneling effect, where only a few people hand delivered the majority of the letters to the target recipient. If you're interested in reading an engaging book that elaborates on this funneling effect, you might want to pick up the book by Malcolm Gladwell, *The Tipping Point*. In it, he proposes that the six degrees phenomenon is dependent on a few extraordinary individuals called "connectors" who have large networks of contacts and friends. Connectors, according to Gladwell, help mediate the connections between a large majority of otherwise weakly connected individuals.

Strong and Weak Ties in a Network

In 1973, Mark Granovetter published a study where he noted that networks have both strong and weak ties. Granovetter noted that strong ties tend to form clusters made up of individuals such as family members, work colleagues, and church members. These strong ties tend to reinforce what (and who) we already know.

Weak ties, on the other hand, are the people who link clusters together. In fact, Granovetter argues, it is the weak ties that are most important for personal advancement (such as getting a job) than the strong ties of family and friendship. The following illustrates the difference between strong and weak ties.

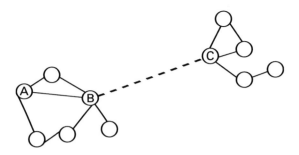

To put it another way, a group of friends who only do things with each other already share the same knowledge and opportunities. But a group of individuals with connections to other social worlds is likely to have access to a wider range of information.

The Strength of Weak Ties

Weak ties play an important role in any number of social activities, including looking for a new job. To get new information about opportunities you wouldn't normally hear about, you need to activate your weak ties. In fact, it is better for individual success to have connections to a variety of networks rather than many connections within a single network.

To support the importance of developing weak ties (which is one of the underlying premises of the introduction-based network described in the Law of 100), there is recent work by Duncan Watts on the small world phenomenon that has far-ranging implications in all areas of science. Watts and his thesis advisor Steven Strogatz have demonstrated how small world networks are common in a variety of different realms, ranging from neurons to power grids.

In their study of small world networks, Watts and Strogatz demonstrated that the addition of a handful of random links can turn a disconnected network into a highly connected one. This is one of the reasons why the introduction-based networking techniques in chapter 8, such as asking to get introduced to "someone who can help you move the ball forward" (as opposed to a specific individual at a specific company) are so effective. The addition of a few more random links (albeit, links that your friends think may be helpful) can increase your success exponentially.

Networking (Re-) Defined

The definition of networking is not that difficult to understand (especially the "extended group of people" part). The scientific foundation as to why networks "work" is also fairly straightforward to understand. What some folks fail to grasp is the spirit of networking, the part about *mutual* assistance and support.

Networking is an ongoing and active pursuit. It's like exercise; you have to do it regularly if you're going to see any results. While the focus of this book is about networking to get the job you really want, there are other results that are less expected. Through contact with new people, you may find yourself getting interested in new hobbies or exploring alternate career paths.

Through the process of being "in transition," I met a number of executives whose networking activities led them to completely different careers. Peter Waller, for example, was formerly the CEO of Taco Bell who had a moment of revelation once he left the company. Much like my own discovery, Peter soon realized "there *are* no CPG (consumer packaged goods) companies in southern California!"

Through networking, the process of talking with and getting to know a diverse group of people, Peter started thinking differently about what he had accomplished in his career and where he would be happy. This led him to set a goal of continuing to live in Southern California. But it also led him to becoming CEO of a start-up that sourced product from China. In fact, Peter did such a great job that the founder decided to rejoin the business and Peter has since moved on to other opportunities—still enjoying the warmth of Southern California.

When we met to discuss my book, Peter confided to me that he probably wouldn't have looked twice at the start-up when he began his search because it wouldn't have seemed relevant to him and he had never worked for a company that small. But during the course of networking and meeting other executives, he started thinking differently about what he had accomplished in the past—which made him think more openly as to what he might do in the future.

One of the other strategies Peter used during his search was to explore how he might get involved in a non-profit organization. I have heard countless stories from executives who have volunteered as a way of building up their network and who later became passionate about the cause they are supporting—whether it's the Surfrider Foundation or the Young Presidents Organization.

Networking can help you create a bigger, richer, and more diverse "personal community." It's not a surprise to anyone that our society is becoming more isolated. And between our jobs and our families, it is difficult to increase the number of people we interact with, even though we may understand intellectually that a broader network can provide us greater perspective in terms of our own lives.

While most senior executives don't live in small towns, we can all make our "personal" towns smaller by getting to know the people we see every day. Your efforts to expand your network will also result in building a stronger community. That community won't only help with your search, but your involvement within your personal community will invariably help others while strengthening the relationships in your network.

Pursuing a lifelong strategy of networking can bring about numerous unexpected and, for lack of a better term, wonderful consequences. As I contend in other parts of this book, networking does not come naturally to me. While I go through periods of extensive travel, I will wear my iPod as I board a flight and, more often than not, will not even make the pretense of introducing myself to the person sitting next to me.

On one flight to Boston, though, I got upgraded to first class and noticed the man sitting next to me reading through brochures from publishers. As I was interested in finding a publisher for my book, I asked him why he had all these brochures. It turned out that his name was Steve Shore and he had written one of the first autobiographies of an autistic man.

I had very limited knowledge about autism and I didn't think I knew anyone affected by it. Steve explained the spectrum to me and we ended up talking for close to an hour. I later read his books and continued to correspond with him. During the course of giving talks about networking, I would stress the importance of creating a diverse network and I would mention the autistic man I'd met who introduced me to a topic I previously knew little about. Invariably, people approach me after the talk to find out more about Steve and to share their stories of their autistic child or relative. By sharing an example about the interesting people you meet networking, I've also been able to help connect people to resources that might help them in their daily life. As I stress in other parts of this book, one of the most important aspects of networking is that it provides a means by which you can provide help to others while also advancing your career and improving your life.

Networking is as much about helping others as it is about helping yourself!

In an interesting twist to the story of my meeting Steve Shore, I later moved from the West Coast to the East Coast and now live one town over from Steve and we continue to share ideas and become closer friends.

From Contact to Relationship: The Five Levels of Networking

Building up relationships doesn't happen overnight. In fact, much like my earlier story about moving to Vermont, it takes effort on your part to *build* new friendships and relationships.

Particularly for senior executives, less than 15 percent of job placement occurs as a result of recruiters and less than 15 percent as a result of ads (which can range from job postings on Monster to ads in the back of the *Wall Street Journal*).

The other 70 percent of jobs for executives come through networking. Other sources suggest 70 percent is a conservative number in terms of networking (and claim that it's more like 90 percent). With numbers like these, it takes someone with a high-risk approach to life to avoid networking when they're looking for their next great opportunity.

Networking, however, requires building stronger relationships with the people you know so that they feel comfortable introducing you to the people they know (this is the foundation of the Law of 100). One of the more interesting ways I've heard someone describe this concept of building relationships is the framework developed by Brad Remillard which he calls Level Five Networking. Brad is a retained executive recruiter and president and cofounder of Impact Hiring Solutions

The Level Five Networking framework gives you a way to think about how to build new relationships—especially when you are in transition and you don't necessarily have the luxury of letting these relationships evolve naturally. Interestingly, most relationships don't "evolve naturally" unless you think about building out your network. No time is better than the present to think about how to move some of your relationships "up the ladder" to a Level Five status.

The Level Five Networking framework can be viewed as a pyramid.

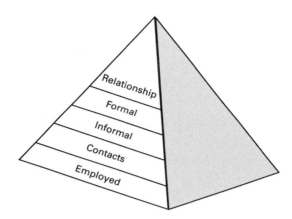

At the base of the pyramid (Level One), you're employed and you perceive networking as offering little value, "you're just too busy."

At the next level, the level most people associate with the phrase "networking," is where you make initial contact with someone. If this occurs at an event, this is typically an exchange of business cards. By itself, this is a low value exchange as your information (the memory of you within the broader context of the event) lasts about ten to fifteen minutes in the other person's mind.

The third level of interaction, which can be considered informal, is characterized by telephone or email contacts. This may have a lasting effect of twenty-four to forty-eight hours.

Level Four is when networking starts creating a greater effect. This is more formalized and includes events such as face-to-face meetings which can make an impression that lasts for up to two weeks. While Level Four events can require time, they help you begin building relationships. Unfortunately, at the early stages of a Level Four relationship, there is a "BUT" associated with any future introductions (i.e., you get referred by someone "BUT" they "don't really know" you).

At the top of the pyramid is the Level Five relationship—a friend for life (or a friend for a career). Relationships that reach this level end up as bonds represented by a strong understanding not just of each other's backgrounds, but your strengths and leadership capabilities on a personal level. There are no "BUTs" when they describe you to another person.

The steps you take to move up the various levels of the pyramid are based on a progressive development of trust. For each person you network with, you need to make an investment of your time. The more you connect with someone, the greater the investment. Very few relationships will reach Level Five. But investing trust and time in your networking efforts will help you create a more effective network for the future.

The base of the pyramid is where you stand when you are employed. While not as safe as your grandfather felt when he got that gold watch for a lifetime of service to the same company, you are still employed.

If you're like many people, though, and you have limited experience in terms of being in transition, you view networking as offering little value to your career or your life. "Between work and family," you think to yourself, "I don't have time to go out for coffee or lunch with someone new." You're just "too busy" to network.

And if you do what you consider to be networking, it consists of meeting with fellow employees, former peers, friends, and colleagues. There is absolutely nothing wrong with this—you should be actively developing those relationships.

Once in a while, though, think about shifting the topic of conversation away from last night's Little League game and toward a business situation where you could use someone's advice or offer to help your friend with a problem that has been vexing her. In this way, you will develop a deeper understanding of each other and, if you ever do find yourself in transition, you'll have a common experience to draw upon when you call your friend to help you strategize toward your new career.

As the work of Milgram, Granovetter, Watts, and others has shown, extending your network to include the "weak" ties can have a powerful impact. In practical terms, this can be achieved by building your relationships in terms of the five level network structure that can help lead you from an initial contact to a lifelong friendship.

CHAPTER 4

LET ME GIVE YOU A BUSINESS CARD

"There are no second chances to make a first impression."

—Anonymous

THE LAW OF 100 is all about introduction-based networking. This means that every new contact you meet is, at some point, meeting you for the first time. That first introduction—whether it was arranged by a friend or it just happened at a networking event or your son's soccer game—is your chance to make a great first impression.

As you'll see later in this chapter, first impressions are mostly based on physical appearance, but the memory of your appearance can be reinforced by other ways you present yourself, such as your business card. The rest of this chapter discusses where you can make those first impressions to help you extend your network more rapidly.

A Brief History of the Business Card

The earliest forms of business cards (referred to as trade cards) were used in seventeenth-century London. They were used as advertising and often included maps to direct the public to merchant stores, as there was no formal street numbering system at the time.

A different type of card also developed during the seventeenth century under the reign of Louis XIV of France. Visiting cards (*visite biletes*) were used to announce a person's arrival at court. Similar to playing cards in size, these were just slightly smaller than the size of a man's hand.

As an adoption from French court etiquette, visiting cards came to America and the rest of Europe. They often included stylish engravings or other features that would make the card memorable. Visiting cards or calling cards were an essential accessory to any nineteenth-century middle-class lady or gentleman.

In the United States, however, there was a rigid distinction between business and visiting cards.

The visiting cards served as tangible evidence of meeting social obligations, as well as a streamlined letter of introduction. The stack of cards in the card tray in the hall was a handy catalog of exactly who had called and whose calls might need to be returned. There were certain fixed rules laid down by society that might apply to a resident in a small town with the same force as in a large city. They did smack of affectation, however, and were not generally used among country folk or working-class Americans.

Business cards, on the other hand, were widespread among men and women of all classes with a business to promote. In terms of etiquette, it was considered to be in very poor taste to use a business card when making a social call. A business card left with the servants could imply that you had called to collect a bill.

While calling cards have only recently gone out of style in the American South, the business card has thrived—although not necessarily everywhere. In the small town where I grew up, I remember as recently as ten years ago I was discussing an upcoming trip to Disneyland with the mayor of an adjoining town, a man who had gone to high school with one of my brothers. I offered to let him stay at a condo I owned in Southern California and he thanked me profusely.

I handed him my business card and he looked as if I had pulled out a gun, and hissed, "Put that away!" I gave him a funny look and he explained, "Only insurance agents and undertakers have business cards around here."

Exchanging business cards is what most people consider to be networking. You meet someone at a business or social function; you somewhat ceremoniously present each other with business cards, tell them briefly about yourself, shake hands, and move along. This brief introduction is commonly referred to as the "elevator speech." The idea is that if you met someone you wanted to do business with in an elevator, you have only a few moments to tell them who you are and what you do.

If it's a social function, your elevator speech might be: "I'm married, have two kids, and live over on Maple Avenue." If it's a business setting, your elevator pitch is that thirty-second infomercial about you or your business. In either event, unless you really stand out from a crowd (if you are the president of the United States or U2's Bono, for example), first impressions are important.

The Importance of First Impressions

First impressions only last ten to fifteen minutes in the other person's mind after they have left you. But that doesn't mean they aren't important. There have been extensive studies that analyze what happens when you first meet someone. Stop and ask yourself—is it what you say, how you say it, or how you look that makes the biggest impression when you meet someone for the first time?

Albert Mehrabian, a UCLA professor, completed research in 1967 showing the significance of nonverbal cues in communications. In an article coauthored with Susan Ferris published in the *Journal of Consulting Psychology*, they concluded that "the combined effect of simultaneous verbal, vocal, and facial attitude communications is a weighted sum of their independent effects—with the coefficients of .07, .38, and .55, respectively."

First Impressions

According to studies, when two people are introduced and have a conversation (or meet to conduct an interview), the following is a breakout of what is most important to the person with whom you're talking.

7 percent *verbal* (the content of what you're saying)
38 percent *vocal* (the way you say it)
55 percent *visual* (how you look)

The immediate translation of this is "dress nicely and speak clearly," whether you're attending a social event or a job interview.

The noted author Tom Wolfe once observed that if you show up at every social function wearing a lime-green suit, you'll stand out and eventually be remembered. Of course, you'll be remembered as the man in the lime-green suit but that's more memorable than the guy with khaki slacks and a polo shirt.

If this all sounds a bit shallow—like you're getting ready for a high school date—that is certainly true. But it is equally true, as the old saying goes, that there are no second chances at making a first impression. You only get to do it once, and it can be so important to improve that there are even consultants who will work with you to help you make a better first impression.

When you first meet someone, introduce yourself appropriately. Listen as much as you talk. Show interest in the other person. Be confident, but also genuine. Make eye contact. Connect.

Most important, though, remember to smile. As previously noted, people form an immediate first (physical) impression of you, usually in under ten seconds, based on some combination of these attributes (in no particular order):

- **+** posture
- **+** walk
- **+** body language
- **+** attire
- **+** physical characteristics
- **+** smile/facial features
- **+** handshake
- **+** grooming
- **+** scent/perfume
- **+** eye contact
- **+** perceived confidence
- **+** perceived comfortableness

In researching first impressions, most of the articles I found were about dating. It was interesting to read a description such as, "Dating is a numbers game and, like it or not, dating occurs in a competitive environment."

Personally, I'm content as long as I don't make a fool out of myself or spill coffee on my shirt. After all, if we're talking about networking (and not strictly about interviewing), it's either one of those random meetings that will only last in someone's mind for fifteen minutes or it's a meeting with someone you've been introduced to and they'll be predisposed to look at you favorably (as long as you don't show up in a lime-green suit).

Formalized Networking Meetings

In the five-level hierarchy of networking presented earlier, Level Two is what most people consider to be networking—going to meetings where you don't necessarily know many people, drinking stale coffee or eating rubbery chicken, and hopefully meeting someone interesting. Level Two contacts, then, are often the result of attending a lot of networking meetings.

These meetings aren't bad—in fact it's with a great sense of relief that you discover there are people even more talented than you who are also out there looking for a job. That is, until you realize that there are people even more talented than you out there looking for *your* job.

There are a variety of networking meetings that are organized specifically for people in transition. I used to get irritated by the phrase "in transition" until I realized that the employed people listening to you feel safer with a word like that. "Unemployed" or "out of work" is just too damn scary to think about when you have a job and three upcoming college tuitions to pay for. Later you'll find out that "in transition" is a better phrase to use than unemployed because getting re-employed is just getting a job. Wouldn't you rather "transition" to a new opportunity?

However, when you're in transition and attending a networking meeting, you're not always feeling your best. Frankly, these can seem like a twelve-step program for the unemployed. At one of these meetings, I remember one man telling the collected group that he didn't get out of bed the day before until 2:30 in the afternoon—he was just too damn depressed. You could watch people nervously navigating somewhere between the island of "At least I'm not that bad (today)" and the shores of "That's nothing compared to the time last month when I got rejected after the fourth round of interviews."

If you approach these meetings on a sort of wholesale networking basis, it's a losing proposition. It becomes collecting and not collaborating. Real networking is about collaboration, and you want to search out meetings where you can find fellow collaborators and leave the collectors behind.

There are a number of places to look for these types of meetings. Outplacement firms will typically host networking meetings for their clients. In Southern California, I was lucky to get involved with a networking group that was supported by a local retained search firm—McDermott & Bull.

Denae Butte, McDermott & Bull's first employee, started the executive networking group soon after the company was formed. Every other week, she shares her energy and enthusiasm with groups of executives in transition. These meetings are typically composed of six to eight executives and consistently change so that you meet some new executives each time

The purpose of the meetings is to expand your network and build relationships to exchange job leads, discover contacts at companies on your target list, and learn new job search strategies.

Meetings like these provide a great opportunity to test drive your approach, and they give you a set of people to bounce ideas off without worrying about looking like a two-headed goat.

Another outcome of these meetings is that they can allay any fears you might have about competing for a job with someone you meet through this process. During my search, there were at least a half-dozen people looking to be CEO of an under-fifty-million-dollar software firm. You'd be hard pressed to imagine a more diverse group of individuals attempting to land the same job. I walked away with the knowledge that when someone hired one of us, it would be clear that they wouldn't have wanted to hire any of the other five.

Industry and Trade Organizations

There's a completely different (and very worthwhile) set of networking meetings that you should investigate as well—trade organizations and other professional groups. These are often attended by executives who are employed and yet are still willing to talk with you. You know they're willing to talk with you because they are out there networking—exactly what you'll still be doing long after you land your next position.

You can gauge whether an organization is appropriate for you after the first meeting—just check the business cards you collected or the attendance roster. If there are peers or more senior executives attending and if the focus of the group is aligned with your career goals, then you've probably found a good organization to get involved with, both during your search and after. If, on the other hand, the majority of people in attendance are administrative assistants for beekeepers, you may want to leave after the honey-mustard chicken and search out a more relevant organization.

Search the Web for "beekeeper" and you'll see there is no shortage of organizational meetings you can attend around the world. If there's a trade, it has an organization. They are typically established for their members' ongoing education and focus on industry trends, legislative issues, and the code of ethics promoted by the industry. In many cases, you'll find local chapters of national organizations where members enjoy interacting with their peers.

You may end up meeting a lot of service providers and, if you owned a business, you might find this irritating ("Thank you, I already have an accountant, attorney, etc."). But, as Terry Goldfarb-Lee noted previously, service providers may be more helpful to you than an executive search firm.

Usually, the attendance at these meetings is too large to allow self-introductions as part of the meeting (that is, each attendee standing up and introducing themselves to the group). That means that attending meetings of the Association for Corporate Growth (ACG) or the Harvard Business School breakfasts requires active participation. You can't be a wallflower and hope to get anything from these gatherings. You need to make an effort to walk up to strangers and introduce yourself. Don't worry, they are there to see their friends (most of whom they met at previous meetings) and meet new people. They are there for the same reasons you are.

When you're trying to meet new people, just remember the golden rule—let the other person talk. A friend once asked me, "What's a salesperson doing when they're not talking?" I didn't know, so she told me. "They're waiting to talk."

By temperament or habit, some people are talkers while others are listeners. Learn to be both. An old Ghanaian proverb says, "We have two ears and one mouth, learn to use them in proportion!" If you are a talker, learn to give enough space for others to speak. If a listener, try to participate more in discussions even if this means simply asking questions. Strategic questioning is just as important, if not more important, as informed comments—and it will make you seem like the smartest person in the room.

As the American poet and humorist Richard Armour once observed, "It is all right to hold a conversation, but you should let go of it now and then."

Networking is a Personal Activity

Association events held annually with a national scope can be a great networking forum and source of job leads within that industry.

Colin Mackenzie attended one of my Law of 100 presentations when I was writing this book and related the following story. "I went to the Financial Services Institute conference in Florida as a means of keeping up with my contacts in the industry. A friend of mine introduced me to the CEO of a company I hadn't been targeting.

"As we made small talk, we discovered that the CEO's wife and I share an interest in ballroom dancing—in fact, the CEO's wife was an instructor and competitor. We ended up having a two-hour 'values' discussion, which was actually an interview in disguise. I later flew to Iowa for a more in-depth interview, and it is one of two opportunities from which I'll choose.

"It's funny how networking is about connecting with people first and then letting other things happen naturally. I've learned that you have to continuously place yourself in environments where you have a chance to succeed...and you will!"

Ranking Your Level Two Contacts

One final note on business cards and networking meetings—you need to be aware of the time you invest in this type of networking. At breakfast and evening gatherings, you can potentially meet dozens of people. Being the good person you are, you'd like to help as many of these people as you can. But if you're focused on succeeding in your transition, you simply won't have time to get in contact with them or—much less—help every one of them. If you're like me, after a few weeks you'll end up with a stack of business cards that you could use to create a little statue of the albatross in "The Rime of the Ancient Mariner." Eventually, after pangs of guilt, you realize you can't possibly respond to most of those people (many of whom you've forgotten anyway).

Here's a tip: when you meet someone, write a ranking on their card between 1 and 3. A "1" is a great contact, someone who may be at a company you've targeted or who knows people you would someday like to meet. Alternately, a "1" may be someone whom you can specifically and immediately help. Whatever your criteria, a "1" is the best possible contact you could meet.

The "2s" are people who might be able to help you out or for whom you might be able to provide some information or assistance. Maybe you worked at one of their target companies or perhaps you've identified a mutual friend.

The "3s" are everyone else. They might be people in different fields (finance, for example, when you're an engineer) or they might be located fifty miles away and are difficult to follow up with.

Be nice to yourself. When you get home from the meeting, sort through your cards and throw away the 3s! Don't even bother to reread the cards, just throw them away. Then you won't be haunted by the stack of cards that go unanswered on your desk.

Level Two networking is what many people think networking is all about—it's not. It is only the starting point for your networking efforts. By attending meetings and meeting new people, you won't necessarily get a referral or a job offer. But you will begin to build a network. By participating with a few organizations, you'll remember to carve out a little time to continually build out your network.

PLEASE ALLOW ME TO INTRODUCE MYSELF

*"Life is like riding a bicycle.
To keep your balance, you must keep moving."*

—Albert Einstein

B ETWEEN THE FIRST TIME YOU meet someone (the Level Two contact) and when you interact one-to-one (a Level Four meeting), you need to start the process of building a relationship. The next two chapters describe Level Three networking, which is all about "moving the ball forward" between Level Two and Level Four. This includes both *contacting* people and *communicating* who you are. The rest of this chapter focuses on the etiquette of the follow-up email or conversation. Even more important than *how* you communicate (which is covered in this chapter) is *what* you communicate.

Chapter 6 addresses how to give a brand identity to the product known as "you."

Following Up after a First Meeting

Once you've made contact with someone, you'll want to follow up with them, and that's what Level Three networking is all about. While exchanging business cards and having a quick chat may last ten or fifteen minutes in another person's mind, starting a dialogue through a phone call or email will have a lasting effect from twenty-four to forty-eight hours. This is the beginning of your deeper networking process.

Whether you're contacting an old friend or following up with someone you met at yesterday's networking event, you should follow some basic rules of etiquette when writing an email or making a phone call. You want the recipient to understand quickly who you are, why you are writing, and why they should be interested in reading your email.

A Short Guide to Email Etiquette

Your writing should be clear, simple (without being simplistic), and human. There are hundreds of books and websites devoted to writing business letters that provide numerous tips and templates. The following notes are just a few things to keep in mind when writing or calling someone.

Find a Style That Works for You

Be creative, positive, and genuine. Avoid anything canned or trite. Your honesty and sincerity will come through. The best emails have a conversational tone. One of the first things new sales associates learn is that people buy from people. Don't write like you're some kind of detached telemarketer reading a script. Be engaging and show your personality.

Be Clear

Keep your writing short, factual, and to the point. Don't write more than one page in length, unless there is some compelling reason to make it longer. Put yourself in the reader's shoes—you have some information or questions for them. Being polite means getting those things out of the way as quickly as possible.

We are all very busy, and our time is precious. Studies show that busy people do not like to read beyond the first few paragraphs. If your email is too long, there is a good chance it will be dumped in a "read later" folder, which often ends up never getting read.

Think of the window that opens for the email when you're writing. Most people will scan what's above the fold (the first paragraph or two), so you need to make your point quickly if you expect them to read the rest of your email. Remember, you're making contact, not telling your life story.

Throughout your email, use short sentences and don't let paragraphs exceed three or four sentences. This should help it flow smoothly and it also makes you stick to the point.

Keep It Simple

Simple means "words of one syllable," as my friend Scott Zahn likes to say. Plain English is clear English. It is simple and direct but not simplistic or patronizing. Using plain English doesn't mean your email is dull—it just means that it's easy to understand.

Use active verbs instead of passive verbs. For example, write "I created…" instead of "I was responsible for the creation of…" This makes your writing clearer, more powerful, and more precise. Once you write your email (or any document), go back and reread it. And while you're reading, pick up a copy of Strunk and White's *Elements of Style*. This book is so useful it should be issued to everyone when they get their driver's license.

Getting Attention

Use the subject line like a headline. Do not write a one-word subject line like "Hi" or the recipient might think your email is spam. Try something like "Follow-up from networking meeting."

Write a clear and strong opening to your email. Your first goal is to gain your reader's attention. It's an important principle of effective writing to put the most important information first. Your opening paragraph is both the headline and the lead for the message that follows in the rest of the letter.

Be sure your opening paragraph sets the right tone for your email. Be direct and use your words positively so your reader has a good impression from the beginning. Decide what the most important information is—and put it in your first paragraph. Don't be afraid to start your letter strongly.

Call to Action

If the average business communication starts poorly, then it invariably finishes poorly. In the last paragraph, make sure the reader knows what needs to happen next. Ask for the appointment or whatever else drove you to write the email.

Check Spelling and Grammar

This should be common sense, but it still needs to be stressed. Sending a letter with obvious misspellings and grammatical mistakes looks sloppy and unprofessional. If you do this, the recipient can't really be blamed for seeing this as an indication of how you do other things.

Don't Overthink It

Yes, there are a lot of books about how to write letters, how to communicate effectively, etc. Just remember that your email has a specific purpose—whether it's to thank someone, provide some information, or set up a meeting. Be direct and clear and you'll be successful.

The email follow-up is an important step to go from an initial contact with someone to the start of building a relationship. When you're first sending an email to someone, you should be prepared to attach a biography to give them a better idea of who you are and what you've accomplished. Think of your biography as an advertisement for you. Many people think of a resume as a promotional tool. But a resume is too formal. It is structured by buckets of time rather than by strengths and accomplishments. A resume looks backwards at your career. A biography, on the other hand, can paint a forward-looking picture of what you will accomplish in your next leadership role.

The next chapter will provide you with some ideas about how to write your biography and even more important, how to create your personal brand! While the email follow-up is the *mechanism* to move from first meeting someone to getting together for a deeper discussion, the biography will provide the *content* for that discussion. It will help the other person understand why you should both get together and how you might help each other.

BECOMING A BRANDED PRODUCT

*"Even if you're on the right track,
you'll get run over if you just sit there."*

—Will Rogers

ONE OF THE MOST IMPORTANT realities you need to face when you are in transition is that "you" are a "product." You don't have to just get comfortable with this idea—you need to embrace it heartily. For the people who know you, they already see you as a great human being (and even enjoy hearing about your vacation plans). But when you're meeting people during your transition, you need to focus on presenting yourself differently—as a superior product with unique features that can help your future employer's business succeed at a higher level.

Of course, you're the product of your parents, who met through some form of an introduction and whose raw materials were combined to create the physical product which is you. I don't think it's critical at this juncture to go into a more detailed explanation of how this all occurred, but I remember talking to a nine-year-old boy several years ago who was just being taught about human reproduction. He had a confused look on his face as he told me that "I understand what the egg is and what the sperm is and that when they get together, a baby is made. But I still don't understand—how?" The "how" of things is always the most difficult to answer.

Much like our young friend, you are filled with experiences from your early life; and in this way you are also a product of your environment. In that way, in terms of your physical being as well as the present "who you are," most of us accept being considered a product because it is inarguable. But many people chafe at the thought that once they joined the workforce, they became a business entity (measured by profit and loss and all the other metrics associated with running a business). And the number one priority of that business is to promote the product called YOU, a product that, if not managed well, can become commoditized.

Avoiding Commodity Status and Becoming a Brand

When you start to think about yourself as a product, think about how you would like to be perceived and promoted. For example, what could be more of a commodity than the coffee bean? People who harvest the beans and sell it on a commodities market make about a dollar per pound, which translates into one or two cents per cup. When a manufacturer takes those beans and roasts, grinds, and packages them, the price can jump to something between five and twenty-five cents per cup. If you brew the coffee and sell it at a corner diner, you can get fifty cents or a dollar per cup. But if you package the product really well and become creative in how you present it (like Starbucks has), people will pay anywhere from two dollars to five dollars per cup.

Humans aren't necessarily as commoditized as the lowly coffee bean. But if you've achieved a certain executive position or level in the business world, you've obviously got the raw goods to be differentiated from all your competition. With the same core product, it then depends upon how you package and present yourself as to whether you're perceived as a commodity or a highly prized serving that commands a premium.

Back in the '90s, the high-tech world rewarded businesses that often only had an idea of a product. The buzz was always about "exit strategies" and "big scores"—windfalls that would make winning the lottery seem insignificant. Businessmen and women in other industries jealously watched (and sometimes jumped to join) this glorious promise of riches. And then, like some bad NASCAR nightmare, it crashed and burned; the aberration went up in flames.

The few survivors competed with great products—highly differentiated, useful, and successful in almost any economy. They didn't think about exit strategies, they thought about long-term value. Most successful companies realized they were in a marathon and not a hundred-meter dash.

Marathon or Sprint?
Think about the difference between a marathon and a sprint the next time you are offered a new position—either within your company or during your transition. Are you taking a job that you may not really want for a "quick hit" or can you see yourself enjoying a marathon run in that role?

It should be clear to you that your career is your "business" and the number one product is you! The importance of branding this "product that is you" cannot be overemphasized. The world continually bombards us with advertisements, special promotions, and daily media events. With your unique product, you need to compete against a wide variety of other well-qualified job seekers who also have a unique product.

Branding for a Marathon and Not a Sprint

Think of us all as snowflakes. Only under a microscope can you discern whether you like one pattern more than another. When people meet you, they won't have the time to take out a microscope to figure out whether they like what you're offering—they need to know quickly what you're about. They can only know this if you have a distinguishing brand!

Branding is about setting yourself apart from the crowd in a memorable way that can be immediately understood. Brands provide us with shortcuts for making decisions. They create an impression and an identity that tells people immediately who you are.

A good brand is short, action-oriented, a bit provocative, and can be linked to the unmet need of a prospective employer. It should not be so general that it can describe anyone—your brand needs to describe you. In order to find the language to describe who you are, there are some interesting exercises you can do to help you define your brand.

Truth in Advertising

One of the first things you can do to get your creative juices flowing is the "100 Things" exercise. Take out a pencil and a piece of paper and write down a hundred interesting facts about yourself that someone wouldn't ordinarily learn about you in an initial casual conversation. This will help you discover some things about yourself that you can later work into your brand (if it's appropriate). If you need some examples, try doing a Google search on "100 things about me." The first time I did this, there were 147,000 hits; the last time I did it, there were 451,000 hits.

That doesn't mean, however, that all of these things will be interesting to everyone (or even that you should publicly confess some of them). As you review your list, put yourself in your audience's seat on the other side of the desk. As you work through creating your brand, your biography, your promotional material, you need to balance two forces:

+ Be true to yourself and what you want.
+ Be interesting to your audience and responsive to what they want.

One way to interpret (or internalize) this concept is to first think about how you can best meet what they need. Even if you can do that effectively, though, you need to apply the second test of whether you will enjoy the role and be challenged. Accepting what someone else needs against your better judgment just postpones your achieving success.

Avoiding the Resume

The next activity to undertake when developing your brand is to create a biography. A biography is a very different document than a resume.

Resumes don't "sell" the product that is you. Obviously, you need one when people ask for it (especially when they're in the human resources department), but the resume by itself won't get you a job. I'll confess right now that while I have submitted resumes in my life, every person I've ever worked for asked for my resume as a formality at the end of the hiring process—not during the time I was being evaluated.

In many circles it's understood that the more senior your position, the less your resume presents a clear picture of your talents. Resumes should be viewed more as follow-up sales literature (highlighting features and benefits) than promotional material to interest the buyer (or hiring manager). Resumes rarely have what sales professionals refer to as a "compelling value proposition." The resume's job is to be your Joe Friday, presenting "just the facts, ma'am."

Your biography, on the other hand, is a way to get in front of more people. A resume says, "I'm looking for a job," but a biography says, "I have some very important skills and accomplishments." If someone thinks about you for the twenty-four to forty-eight hours after you write them an email, they may forward your biography to someone else they know. The end result may be a call for you to "come in and let's talk." A resume will rarely get you that call.

The biography should intrigue the reader and demonstrate what you know rather than what job titles have been on your business card. While a resume "tells," the role of your biography is to "show" your skills and accomplishments. Your biography can be especially helpful if you're trying to change industries because it highlights broad-based skills that are transferable to any business. These are typically "soft" skills associated with various aspects of leadership, project management, or sales and marketing.

As an aside, if for some reason you feel compelled to respond to job ads, your biography can be a great starting point instead of sending a resume. One reason to avoid sending a resume in the first place is that resumes automatically get routed to the human resources department, and human resources managers don't make hiring decisions. Their job is to screen people out, and in many companies, HR stands for hiring resistance.

Your Personal Agent

As you sit down to write your biography, think about your personal agent (your own Leigh Steinberg or Scott Boras) sitting across from the CEO of the company you want to join. If you want the top job, then just picture him with a board member. The CEO leans back in his chair and says, "Leigh, this player has an interesting background, how would she help our company?"

A question like this puts Leigh (and you) in the driver's seat. You can respond to this question by highlighting the skills and expertise you possess that can help the CEO solve his problems or grow his business. This is important because if you're interviewing for an executive position, those are the two things you can do. You can solve problems (which can sometimes be translated as cutting costs or creating more efficiencies in the company) or you can help grow revenue. It hardly seems worth calling out, but revenue growth is of interest to every executive you'll meet.

By thinking about your agent presenting you to the CEO, you can write it as if it were a news report about the most promising candidate the CEO will meet this year. Much like a news story, you want to quantify both your previous accomplishments as well as how you will bring benefit to your future employer. Because the CEO is a busy individual, you want to keep it to one page.

In writing your biography and creating your branding statements, you are trying to help people understand and relate to the uniqueness of who you are and what you want. This will evolve over several iterations—especially as you test your brand messages—first with friends and family and later in the field, where it will matter the most.

How to Create a Compelling Biography

To help you get started on your biography, I've enlisted the help of my friend Carleen MacKay, who, as an executive coach, gave me a good punch in the nose to get me to work on what I really wanted in my career. Carleen's most recent work is in the "third career" for those managing a transition after turning fifty.

In terms of the skeleton of a good professional biography, Carleen notes that few good rules exist that were not meant to be broken. But that doesn't mean that you should break rules just because you can. If you do break rules, do it consciously and for effect.

In terms of the technical aspects of your biography, you should use a twelve-point font (a fourteen-point font for titles, etc.) and select an easy-to-read font such as Times New Roman or Arial. Don't get too cute with the effects available in Microsoft Word and try to limit even the use of bold fonts or italics. You need your biography to exhibit the same professionalism that you do.

To create visual impact, design for eye appeal. Use the white space on the page liberally—it's the music between the notes that makes the symphony—and the white space between sentences that attracts the mind's eye. Another tip for designing for the eye is to limit the length of any paragraph to a maximum of six lines, even if you end up breaking the usual rules of grammar.

As mentioned previously, keep your biography short (less than one page). Four or five well-crafted paragraphs are sufficient for most biographies. And when you're done, don't edit your own work. Typos are glaringly noticeable to everyone but the writer.

Now that these technical details are out of the way, it's time to commit YOU to paper. Remember to write to a targeted audience and not to yourself. At the same time, remain true to yourself and your message. Don't portray yourself as an entrepreneur (because you think entrepreneurs are getting hired) if you're a risk-averse *Fortune* 500 executive. You'll be happier being who you really are. Over the course of the following pages, Carleen shares some advice about what language makes up the body of a good biography. This is not only good advice for words you might use to describe yourself, but these examples can help you identify your strengths and establish some of the criteria that should be met in your next executive role.

Creativity

○ Yes   ○ No

Are you especially *creative*? Do others remark on this quality? Are you known for seeing many possibilities to solve a problem?

When you choose to describe your *creativity*, consider using versions of the following action words and phrases:

Architect	Inspire
Artist within	Intuitive
Author	Invent
Conceptual	Original
Create	Originate
Imagine	Perceive
Ingenious	Unique
Innovate	

An example from a biography to convey *creativity*:

"Architect of experiential learning concept, model, and curriculum for people who must learn to manage their careers in a rapidly changing and exciting new world."

Entrepreneurial

○ Yes   ○ No

Would you describe yourself as *entrepreneurial*? Will you take risks for the sake of your strongly held ideas? Would others describe you as an ideal partner for a daring business venture?

When you choose to describe your *entrepreneurial* life skills, consider using versions of the following action words and phrases:

Action-oriented	Influence change
Challenge	Invent
Change	New
Compete	Overcome obstacles
Curious	Passion
Dare	Persuade
Energetic	Pilot
Fast	Produce
First to think of	Risk-friendly

An example from a biography to convey your *entrepreneurial accomplishments*:

"Founded and ran a successful apparel manufacturing firm. Led the firm from startup through buyout by a large retail conglomerate."

Followed by: "Pioneered ways of exploring new opportunities in…"

Future-Focused

○ Yes   ○ No

Would you describe yourself as *future-focused*? When new ways present themselves as solutions to old problems, are you the first to adapt to a new way of doing something? Do you have a good sense of the future?

When you choose to describe your *future focus*, consider using versions of the following action words and phrases:

Adaptable	Envision
Big-picture	Trendsetter
Proactive (overused)	Explore
Challenge the past	Future-focused
Champion new ideas	Visionary
See patterns and	Insightful
meanings	Looks forward
Change the world	

An example from a biography to convey *future-focus:*

"Conceptualized, designed, and built three technology-rich molding plants in an industry that does not readily embrace changes in technology."

Followed by: "A key to operating all institutions in the future is learning how to take advantage of technology."

Interpersonal Relationships

○ Yes   ○ No

Are you driven by *interpersonal relationships?* Is it important to you to be part of a team? If others were asked, would their first inclination be to describe you as someone they would want on their team?

When you choose to describe your *interpersonal* life skills, consider using versions of the following action words and phrases:

Collaborative	Develop
Community	Empathy
Contribute	Guide
Cultivate	Help

Inspire	Resolve
Liaison	Synergy
Mediate	Teach
Mentor	Team developer
Relate	

An example from a biography to convey *interpersonal skills* or *ability to influence others*:

"Helped people to change their attitudes of fear and uncertainty to excitement and anticipation of the newly restructured organization."

Organization

○ Yes   ○ No

Do you bring a strong sense of *organization* when completing projects? Is your ability to efficiently structure project tasks what you are known for by others?

When you choose to describe your *organizational* life skills, consider using versions of the following action words and phrases:

Accomplish	Determine
Assemble	Exact
Check	Focus

Infinite care	Organize
Initiate	Plan
Install	Schedule
Integrate	Support
Maximize	Precise outcomes
Methodize	

An example from a biography to convey *organizational* strength:

"Monitored firm's managed care health insurance programs. Obtained and thoroughly reviewed proposals. Conducted a cost/benefit analysis of finalists' proposals."

Sales

○ Yes   ○ No

Do you like to influence others to your way of thinking? Does it give you a thrill to compete and win? Would others describe you as one of the best salespeople they know? You may wish to describe your natural interest and abilities in *sales* or customer service.

When you choose to describe your *sales-centered* life skills, consider using versions of the following action words and phrases:

Assertive

Challenge

Compete

Confident

Disciplined
approach

Fearless

Quantifiable record
of results

Self-starter

Think fast

Win

An example from a biography to convey *sales* strength:

"Recruited the division's new product go-to-market team. Created systematic selling approach that resulted in team exceeding first year targets. Rewarded when entire team invited to President's Club to celebrate most successful product launch in company's history."

Systems Orientation

○ Yes   ○ No

Can you concentrate for long periods of time? Do you precisely work the kinks out of systems until tasks are complete? If so, you may seek to communicate your strong *systems orientation*.

When you choose to describe your *systems-oriented* life skills, consider using versions of the following action words and phrases:

Accuracy	Follow-through
Analytical	Logical
Concrete	Objective
Data-oriented	Process-driven
Factual	Reflective
Focused	Systematic

To convey *systems orientation:*

"Steadfastly used a systems approach to manage the merger of five confectionary businesses."

Followed by: "Measured the impact of these new ideas through the kinds of pen-and-pencil techniques still found in most laboratories today."

Social or Spiritual Values

○ Yes   ○ No

Some people are driven by *social or spiritual values.* If values are your driving force, you most likely have a strong need to help others and yourself achieve altruistic goals. Does this sound like you most of the time?

When you choose to describe your *social or spiritual values*, consider using versions of the following action words and phrases:

Authority
Balanced approach
Spirit or spiritual
Belief systems
Challenge
Social contribution
Creativity
Diversity
Self-confident
Environment

Ethics
Self-actualized
Flexibility
Helping others
Recognition
Independence
Life purpose
Philosophy*
Principled

If you have a personal philosophy, consider using it in your biography. For example, Linda Ellerbee wrote, "Change is one form of hope; to risk change is to believe in tomorrow." A retiree wrote, "I wanted to do something to lose sleep over again." Can you see how, when woven into a biography, these statements— or philosophies—tell a reader a lot about the writers?

✻ ✻ ✻

By now, you're probably wondering how you'll know when you have a great biography. According to Carleen, there are three tests that should tell you whether you've written a truly great biography.

When you have written a creative and truthful document that *demonstrates who you are* in a compelling format that intrigues the audience so they want to know more, you'll have met one test of a great biography.

When your biography helps you to stay *focused on the central theme* of your unique career and your career's purposeful journey, you'll have met the second test of a great biography.

When your biography clearly demonstrates the wonderful gifts you bring to others *from their perspective*, you'll have met the final test of a great biography.

Your New Branded Business Cards

Once you've written your biography, which should go a long way toward defining your brand, you can start creating other tools that will support your brand. One is your business card, that leave-behind during an initial meeting and often at all subsequent meetings.

The first business card I used when I was in transition was professionally printed (and really, really boring).

John M. Davies
Executive Management

JMDeight@gmail.com
eFAX: 509/461-2263

949/640-7097
(cell) 949/500-5938

You can see that there's absolutely no risk taken here (and no personality). I'm not suggesting that you go out and print pink scented cards for your transition from linebacker to line management, but you do need to consider the impression your business card will make when you hand it to someone and when it's on their desk at home (or in their hand as they try and remember which of the twenty people they met you were).

There are some very easy things you can do to make your business cards stand out and be more effective. First, with the exceptional quality of printers that can be purchased for under a hundred dollars, you should print customized business cards at home. It will obviously be more expensive than the free business cards offered by companies like VistaPrint.com. But printing your own cards will pay off in many ways.

As I described in the previous chapter, first impressions count. Even more so is the impression someone gets if they pick up your card later and try to remember who you are. I ended up printing a few different cards, depending upon what type of meeting I was attending. In fact, I landed a consulting engagement because I printed a card with the phrase "Turning Products into Profits" under my name instead of a hoped-for title.

The Law of 100, Inc.
Turning Products into Profits

John Davies
Co-Conspirator

Cell 949.500.5938

www.lawof100.com   john.davies@lawof100.com

The person I gave the card to (who I met through networking) was so intrigued by the phrase that he hired me for an ongoing consulting assignment. I never dared to ask him what he thought the phrase meant, but few CEOs will pass by someone who can help them make a profit (especially in undercapitalized software companies).

As you can see, I put the Law of 100 where a company's name would normally go. As my title, I put "Co-Conspirator" under my name (I'll describe the role you and your network play as co-conspirators in detail later). That title at least gets a smile from someone and usually provides an icebreaker for a conversation—a great thing to have in a crowded room.

One man who did this to great effect is Andy Lesko, a self-certified "De-Engineer." Andy made up the title De-Engineer to describe a detailed road map for developing and introducing new products. Whenever I've attended a gathering where Andy is, there was always someone engaged in conversation with him—usually because they wanted to know what a De-Engineer did for a living.

You can buy blank business card stock for your home printer at any office products store. If they don't include software in the package, you can download templates from a number of websites (if you use Microsoft Word, you already have some basic templates). If you're interested in something with more elaborate templates, you can buy relatively inexpensive business card formatting software from your local electronics or office megastore.

It might take you a few tries to get it right, but the benefit of custom printing your business cards shouldn't be underestimated. How you thought about yourself and what you were searching for at the start of your transition may be very different from where you are three months later. Printing your business cards on demand gives you the flexibility to change how you present yourself at different times and to different audiences.

At first, it may seem difficult to think of yourself in the same terms as the products that line the aisles of a grocery store. But the executives who are hiring often find themselves as confused as I am when I confront shelf after shelf of shampoo—and not one bottle looks like the one my wife sent me to pick up. It's your job to promote what makes you distinctively different and you need to make this instantly recognizable. Your unique brand is what will help you stand out in a crowd in a networking event or a final interview.

LET'S GET TOGETHER

"The only way to have a friend is to be one."

—Ralph Waldo Emerson

W HILE MEETING PEOPLE AT social mixers is the conventional view of networking, personal meetings are where the "work" in networking gets done. Now that you've started to develop your brand, you can use it to help people understand how they might help you *and* how you might be able to help them.

The final two levels of the networking pyramid are where relationships are built. While this requires a greater investment of time, the payoff is greater as well. The following chapter provides some tools for making those first meetings productive as well as some guiding principles for building out your network. The easiest and most important of these is to thank everyone who helps you along the way.

Meeting Your New Networking Friends

Networking really starts to pay off when it gets more formalized—that is, when you're meeting face-to-face. This might be early-morning coffee, breakfast, lunch, or other breaks in the day. When you're working hard at this you'll feel like you're floating (and you literally will if you drink another iced tea or coffee), but these meetings are what networking, and your search, are all about.

Face-to-face meetings can make an impression that lasts for up to two weeks. This is the greater reward for greater investment and that is why you need to be prepared for these meetings.

It's been mentioned several times already, but networking is about giving, and the first thing you can give someone you are going to meet is a positive, relaxing experience. This is easy because all you have to do is think about how you like to be treated and do that for them.

Pick a Quiet Place

Pick a place to meet where you know you can have a conversation. Starbucks could have a line item in their annual report for the amount of networking that contributes to their bottom line, but not all Starbucks are created equal. Some are rock 'n' roll and some are more business oriented. If at all possible, suggest meeting places where you know you'll be able to hear the other person talk without constantly asking her to repeat herself.

Pick a Time That Fits Their Schedule

When you are meeting with someone who is working, early morning, lunch, or after work are typically the best times. This leaves mid-morning and mid-afternoon to meet with other executives in transition or to make phone calls. Remember, emails can be done any time of the day or night, but there are only so many hours that you can call or meet face-to-face with people.

Be Early

It might be fashionable to show up late to a cocktail party, but not for a business appointment. Take into account that traffic doesn't flow at the same speed every day. Even when you take a train, the one day it doesn't run on time might be the morning of your meeting.

Make Yourself Visible

Before the meeting, you might want to send a picture of yourself via email or a note that you'll be carrying a bright green binder. Then you won't have to walk around the coffee shop asking everyone if they're Fred.

Build Rapport

Now that you've created a positive environment in which to meet them, start an open, genuine, and honest conversation with them. The best starting point is to either recall events from your past relationship or talk about the mutual contact who introduced you.

Don't Ask for a Job

The one thing you want to make abundantly clear, however, is that you are not asking them for a job and that you don't expect them to tell you about any opportunities. Your goal (as well as that of the person you're meeting with) is to start learning about each other's background in detail. This is the beginning of building a foundation of trust.

This is not to say you want to completely disregard that you're meeting for a reason. You should present a clear picture of your background and what you're looking for—both in terms of target position and target companies. And you should ask the person you're meeting with to do the same.

Tools for Your Networking Meeting

When you meet with someone, especially someone new, you need to bring some tools with you. The best tools to bring with you are your biography (which you should email to them in advance) and a condensed version of your resume that can fit on two-thirds of a page.

The condensed resume provides jumping-off points so that you can "tell a story" about your work history. It is important to tell stories because that's what people remember. If you tell about some unique event that occurred when you were the night shift receiving manager at the start of your career (maybe the time the Brinks truck backed up and started unloading money on your dock), there's a much better chance they'll remember that.

The more specific you are the better. If you tell someone that the driver unloaded $585,000 before he realized it was the wrong dock, you've doubled the chance of your companion remembering the story. They'll probably ask you how big 585 grand is; and when someone starts asking questions, they start internalizing the story.

The alternative is, "I worked at Big Co. as the receiving manager during the summer. We received boxes of stuff and put them away." It's a good bet that no one will remember what you said thirty seconds after you said it—unless they worked at Big Co. at some point in their life.

As with the example above, make sure to illustrate your stories with quantified achievements and quality results. Just as your resume should be stocked with great quantified achievements (e.g., "I grew our revenue by $5 million, which was a 35 percent increase for the division"), your conversation should as well.

During a first meeting with someone, it shouldn't be your goal to present your life history. The abbreviated format of your resume will help you focus on presenting key achievements, but the real focus of the meeting should be on the future.

Use the bottom third of your abbreviated resume to identify your target position, your target industry, and your target companies. A target position is the specific name of the job that you really want. It's more helpful if it's the title used in your target industry.

Once you've named that title and the industry, start listing the companies where you would like to do that job. This gives you both something to talk about—do they know anyone at those companies, do they know any similar types of companies, etc. While these might not be the companies that employ you, they are the companies that will help you get a job because they're helping you drive a conversation to expand your opportunities.

About 75 percent of all jobs are found through a proactive approach (targeting companies for existing jobs or pending/created jobs), whereas a reactive approach (responding to ads, websites, agencies, and recruiters) accounts for only 25 percent of the jobs. By creating a target list of companies, you are identifying all of the companies that match your criteria. The target list is an effective networking tool because it helps your networking contact understand your market quickly.

A target list is typically narrowed down by location, industry, and size (number of employees). You should review your target list on a weekly or biweekly basis. One useful reference to help you do this is *The Book of Lists*. This yearly periodical presents a list of the top companies in a particular location and industry. You can find a number of lists on the Web at www.bizjournals.com.

"I Think He'd Be Good, But…"

Getting together for one-on-one networking is all about starting to build trust. This is where you learn about other people's backgrounds and they begin to learn about your strengths and accomplishments. This all requires time, and there's still one aspect of reaching this level that will make you want to work harder to know them even better.

Once you start networking face-to-face with new people, there is only one word that stands between you and their network of individuals who can help you in your search. It's not a really complicated word, in fact it's only three letters. It is, however, the most powerful word they use. That word is "but…"

"But" is the qualifier of any relationship, the "get out of jail free" card that everyone carries with them. It protects its user and keeps them safe.

"Yes, I do think Jack could do a great job as your new vice president of sales and I think you should really meet him…but I have to confess I've never actually worked with him in the same company. I do know him from the industry, though, and no one speaks badly of him."

Ouch! It's not clear what's worse for Jack—getting that recommendation or not. However, until you know someone better, you will get a limited, cautious referral. The only way to combat this is to get to know them better.

If you volunteer for an organization, this can occur as you work on committees with other volunteers. They get to know the kind of work you're capable of even though they haven't been employed by the same company. If you're developing these relationships through networking, though, you need to set aside time to get to know the people you are networking with. You need to meet them more than once if you're going to build a relationship.

Friends for Life: Building Level Five Relationships

Very few relationships get to the fifth level of the pyramid These are friends who will be with you throughout your career. When you reach this point, people have a strong understanding of not only your background, but also your strengths and leadership capabilities on a personal level. There are no "buts" when they describe you to another person. These come from common experiences and a bond of trust that is built over time. If the result of face-to-face networking can last up to two weeks, this type of relationship should last for months or years—many for a lifetime.

Is it worth it? In a word, yes. Even if these do not become "family" relationships and they remain on a business level, they are extremely important. These are people who will not only refer you to new opportunities, these are people who will sell your capabilities on a personal level. They will have no hesitation in their voice when they describe you.

Finally, the biggest benefit of developing a new community (building up strong relationships) is the opportunity to get to know some really great people. Truly fascinating people you never would have had the good fortune to meet if you hadn't started to develop your community.

A New Definition of Networking: Helping Others, Trust, and Mutual Respect

You don't need to make a hundred new Level Five friendships to get the job you really want, but in building your own List of 100, it can't be completely populated with Level Two contacts either. Between Level Three (phone and email conversations) and Level Five (friends for life, who I like to call my co-conspirators), there will be a range of new introductions that help you move your search along.

At its foundation, networking is about:

+ Helping others, and
+ Mutual respect.

If you provide those two things, you will reap greater rewards. It may take a little longer to build your network, but in the end, you'll really have a "network" that will keep working for you throughout your professional career.

To illustrate why it's important to show mutual respect (or common courtesy), I'll tell you a story that happened to me before I came up with the idea for the Law of 100. I met a man; we'll call him M. M sent me the following email:

We didn't get a chance to speak at the exec lunch, but I noted your <previous company> experience. Thought it might be worth a conversation to exchange lies and other info. Live in Orange County? If so, how about coffee?

I had worked at my previous company for eighteen years and so this was intriguing. Had he worked there? What sort of lies were there to exchange? I didn't remember him from the meeting (I probably wrote a "3" on his business card and tossed it when I got home). We agreed to meet at a family restaurant for a cup of coffee.

M is a tall, confident man. He can fill a room (only at first I hadn't realized what he was filling it with). We made small talk while I tried to figure out if he was connected to my previous company in some way I hadn't noticed during all those years (it turned out he had interviewed there at one point with my partner). He then asked me what I was looking to do next and I told him I wanted to run a small software company.

He had a similar goal. He immediately gave me the names of two people who he thought I should talk with. The two businesses he described sounded dodgy at best, but they were two more people to call. I didn't know at the time to ask for introductions. While I stared into my coffee, I wondered why he was pointing me to these people when they potentially had a job he wanted. M then blurted out, "Okay, I've given you two names. What two names are you going to give me?"

I immediately felt uncomfortable. I hadn't learned enough about networking to know why, but I knew this request wasn't right. This wasn't one friend trying to help another; this was an accounting ledger. It wasn't just a numbers game he was working on. It was rude.

M did not get an introduction to anyone in my trusted network. In fact, he got a couple of useless introductions. I had a pang of guilt about this at first. Did these people deserve to be subjected to M? Probably not, but they've since forgiven me.

Always Say Thank You

M didn't get it. There's etiquette to networking. That's why you need to consider the different levels of relationships and understand at which level you are with the various people you know. You have to build a relationship of trust before you can expect to be trusted.

Etiquette is not aggressively networking at social gatherings. Someone who suddenly begins passing out business cards at a party or their daughter's soccer game is going to make just about everyone very uncomfortable.

Etiquette is also not disingenuous. Sending someone a resume to explain "how I can help" is not offering help. It's looking for a job.

The cardinal sin of networking, though, the most neglected rule of etiquette, the one thing that will knock all your efforts off the track, is not following up with a thank-you.

Networking is about mutual respect. Always follow up any action you take with a short note of thanks. You can include your current status as of your last meeting or phone call. You can include a follow-up to something they told you. But first things first—you need to say thank you.

Thank you for meeting with me.

Thank you for contacting them for me.

Thank you for the introduction.

As the last several chapters have shown, creating a network to find a job you'll love requires you to progressively build trust with the people you meet. By understanding how relationships are built, you can now start applying the Law of 100 to your job search.

IT'S NOT WHO YOU KNOW, IT'S WHO THEY KNOW

"In particular, the more your friends know each other, the less use they are to you in getting a message to someone you don't know."

—*Six Degrees*, by Duncan J. Watts

THE LAW OF 100 STARTS HERE. To get to this point, you've done all the ground work. You have a biography and a resume. You've created your Job/Contact Matrix and filled it out completely (and you know a lot more people than you thought you did). You also know the way to look at your relationships with others and how to drive some of those relationships to a higher (or deeper) level.

Most important, though, you now have a solid idea about what you are pursuing. The only other important thing you need is an open mind. As you progress on your journey of meeting one hundred new people, the landscape will change. Being open to new opportunities will make for a more fulfilling journey and will lead to greater success.

Don't mistake open-mindedness and the concept of a "fulfilling journey" with some granola-infused new age rhetoric. During your transition you will meet people who will tell you how envious they are and that "you should really enjoy this time off." Refrain from physical violence and realize that:

a) They have either never been in transition, or

b) They have chosen to forget how they felt, or

c) They are delusional.

The fourth option is that they don't have to work, which is a completely acceptable reason for enjoying their transition time as you would yours. What others may fail to grasp is that for you the unemployment rate is not 5.2 percent—it's 100 percent.

According to the Bureau of Labor Statistics (BLS), the average job hunt in 2005—regardless of the salary sought—is seventeen to nineteen weeks. However, you can't assume that your job search will be "average." As you see from recent BLS statistics, almost 20 percent of job searches can take twenty-seven weeks or more.

October 2005	
Total unemployed	100.0
Less than 5 weeks	36.1
5 to 14 weeks	30.4
15 weeks and over	33.5
15 to 26 weeks	14.0
27 weeks and over	19.5

I have talked with numerous executives in transition who identify opportunities that were presented early in their search that they rejected, only to later realize they were potentially rewarding. As many people have learned, it may be that through the process of applying the Law of 100 that you discover a different position or career than you may have envisioned at the outset. This doesn't mean you shouldn't have a defined goal, but you should also bring an open mind.

Quality versus Quantity: It's About Who, Not How Many

As described throughout this book, the Law of 100 is about getting introduced to one hundred new people. This is different than merely getting referrals.

Conventional wisdom or one of the rules of thumb presented to the job seeker is to "always get two referrals" or two new names. This is typically highlighted as a point of leverage where 1 = 3. The 1 is the person you are talking with and 3 is the number of contacts you have when he or she gives you two new names.

The "always get two referrals" approach certainly works in terms of increasing the number of people you meet. But it doesn't necessarily help you find people willing to advance your cause. Particularly with senior executives in transition, meeting new people is more about quality than quantity. This doesn't mean that you don't want to apply metrics to your search (in fact, a later chapter presents a set of metrics you can apply). It means that you should focus on getting quality introductions instead of just getting "net new names."

Think about it like dating. On the one hand, you could go to a social function and meet a dozen new people. On the other hand, your best friend can introduce you to someone that he's already described to you and you agree is worth meeting. Which approach do you think has the higher success rate?

The most important aspect of the Law of 100, then, is the introduction. The means by which you get the introduction—and the way that you get introduced—are both extremely important to your search.

Ask for Bob

As a prelude to picking up the phone and asking for your first introduction, I'll share a story from my college days that revealed to me that it is possible to get in touch with people you would never expect to as long as you try.

It was near the end of the semester and my friends and I just heard the news that Bob Marley had been shot. In Jamaica, the political warfare going on in 1976 during the elections was intense. If he supported either candidate, it would decide the election. He was set to perform a large outdoor concert just before the election. The opposition party ambushed his house to stop him from performing and Bob Marley was wounded by gunfire. Later, after taking a few days to recover, he performed for eighty thousand people to help keep the peace, and then went into exile for eighteen months.

It was the day after he got shot and I told my roommate that we should call him and tell him that we're thinking of him and that we hope he's feeling better. My friends looked at me like I was crazy and so I picked up the phone and dialed information for Jamaica. When someone at the hospital answered, I quickly said, "Put me through to Bob Marley's room, please." I was as surprised as anyone, but the phone started ringing and a voice on the other end said, "Hello?"

"Is this Bob?" I asked.

"No," came the reply. "Bob's sleeping right now. This is Chris, can I help you?"

"No, I just wanted to call Bob and see how he's doing. Please tell him that John Davies called and I hope he's feeling better."

"I'll do that," he said and hung up. I may not have reached Bob Marley, but I did talk with Chris Blackwell.

That was a great day. As one of Bob Marley's peers, Jimmy Cliff, sang:

"You can get it if you really want,
But you must try,
Try and try,
Try and try,
You'll succeed at last."

Just remember to "ask for Bob." In other words, you have to make a call if you want someone to answer their phone. More often than not, you'll be surprised by the result.

The Second-Call Expletive

You've resolved to get high-quality introductions. You've steeled yourself to ask for Bob. You now face the worst call you have to make when you're in transition. This is the dreaded second call to someone you know.

The first call was fine. You probably said something like the following:

"I'm no longer at the company."

"I've decided to pursue an opportunity that's better for me."

"The company has restructured."

And your friend's response was likely filled with empathy:

"While I don't know of anything off the top of my head, I'll keep my ears open."

That first call was great. With the exception of not achieving anything and announcing to the world that you're now unemployed, it really went well.

But time goes by (maybe a week, maybe a month, maybe two months) and you've heard about this "networking thing" and you decide you need to keep in touch with all your primary contacts. This call, the second call, is what many people find to be the hardest call to make. The second-call dynamic can be boiled down to the following exchange.

"Hi, I'm still unemployed."

"Hi," responds the person on the other end of the line. "I still have no idea where you can get a job."

This call is typically uncomfortable for both of you and can be measured in seconds rather than minutes. When the receiver is placed back in the cradle, it is difficult to say who is more relieved: the caller or the person who was called.

The strategy of using the Law of 100 to make this call changes the dynamic completely. With the Law of 100, you'll find you can extend these painful second calls into long-term conversations that provide you with important information and even more important introductions to new people.

The second call has four major goals:

1. Make the person you call comfortable with helping you (get them to join your conspiracy).

2. Arrange an introduction to someone who can help you in your search.

3. Keep talking long enough to get additional information that can help you in your search.

4. Keep a positive networking relationship with the person you call.

The second call (and soon the first call to people you've been avoiding or are meeting for the first time) needs to be filled with positive energy. As mentioned previously, the first goal is to break down the barriers people naturally put up when dealing with something they're uncomfortable with.

The second call isn't uncomfortable because people don't want to help you. It's uncomfortable because they don't know *how* to help you. And when faced with failure (disappointing you because they don't know how to help), they'll try to keep the conversation short. So when they answer the phone and ask you if you're still looking for a job, change the tone of the conversation immediately.

"Yes, I'm still looking, but I'm calling you for a different reason."

Poof! You've just performed a sleight of hand that would make Houdini (or Ricky Jay) proud. You've poured water into their favorite baseball cap, but when you turn it over it's dry! Applause echoes on the line. You've given them a "get out of jail free" card. The person you're calling doesn't have to listen to how hard it is to get a job because *that's not why you're calling.*

 And now, a quick time out for this important message from Politeness Man! Before you start any phone conversation, make sure you show just how much you respect this individual. No matter who you call, always ask, "Is this a good time to talk?"

This is important for two reasons. First—and most important—it's common courtesy. Second—and important for you—it sets the stage for you to work with them for the next five or ten minutes knowing that you won't have to stop in the middle of the conversation.

Asking for the Introduction

Now, why are you calling?

"The real reason I'm calling you is I read this nutty book by a guy who is convinced that if I can get introduced to one hundred new people that I can get any job I want. Now he says I obviously have to be qualified, but..."

Now what are they thinking? When you're sitting down with someone having a cup of coffee and using this technique, you can almost see the calculation going on behind their eyes.

+ 100 people—that's a lot, so that makes sense.
+ Get introduced—sure, that's definitely the best way to meet people.
+ Who do I know?—I bet I can figure out one person I can introduce you to, let me just think for a minute.

The response to this proposition is usually "that makes a lot of sense." Now you haven't just lowered the barriers, you've begun to involve them in your search in a way that helps you and makes them feel good. Once they agree that your approach makes a lot of sense, you need to help them figure out the right person for an introduction. When you buy a house, conventional wisdom says it's a good idea to aim a little higher than you're comfortable with. For introductions, this means aiming for someone who would be a peer of your boss or your boss's boss.

During your early search calls, you might not be as specific. But as I've noted in many other parts of this book, the more specific you are, the more your network can help.

"You know I'm still looking for a position of vice president of operations in the faux fig leaf industry and I'd like to stay in Southern California. But I'm open to other opportunities as well."

You want to help the other person with a focus and open up the conversation. One phrase that can work well during this part of the conversation is: "I'm looking to meet someone who can help me move the ball forward in my search."

But the important thing to reassure them with as you describe your target position or company or geography, is: "I'm just looking for you to introduce me to one new person..."

Everyone feels that they can introduce you to one new person. I have yet to hear of anyone using this technique where they didn't get an introduction. It may not be a great introduction (although you have to remember the earlier advice to not prejudge), but it serves another purpose at this moment in time. It keeps the conversation going.

Extending the Conversation

You've now reached a critical juncture in the

conversation. If your life was an action movie, this is the scene where the kidnapper calls to demand the ransom. The police have the tracer on your phone and you can see the captain drawing his hands away from each other. "Keep him on the line," the hard-nosed detective tells you, "because the longer you can do that, the better chance we have of determining his location."

The location you're trying to determine is the next great point in your career. And the longer you keep your contact on the phone, the more information and ideas he or she will give you. This is the one time that you are "top of mind" and you need to make the most of it. As they try and figure out who the best person is to introduce you to, they will come across other ideas for your search.

"By the way, did you know that Joe went over to Palm Frond Industries to run sales? You should probably call him and see who he knows. Now, let's see who I can introduce you to that you don't already know. My brother-in-law runs a manufacturing plant in Redlands, maybe he'd be good to talk to just in terms of general networking. By the way, there's a retirement lunch for Vera next Thursday. You should join us and then you can try this out on some of the other folks."

Bingo! You've hit the jackpot! Your contact is now a co-conspirator. Funny things happen with co-conspirators. Your search becomes their search. The call creates a positive feeling for both of you, which makes it much easier to pick up the phone and make the next call. And it makes it easy for them to make the introduction for you.

Never Accept a Referral

At this point, you need to guide them as to how to make an introduction. This is important because the phrase you want to avoid is: "You can use my name."

Using someone's name is very different from having them introduce you. Introducing you requires a commitment on their part. It means that they trust you enough to make an introduction. And it means they know the person they will introduce you to well enough to interrupt their day to make the introduction. When you get the offer to "use my name," you need to refocus the conversation to get an introduction.

"I really appreciate you introducing me to George. You know, instead of me just mentioning your name, do you think you could write him an email and copy me on it? That way I'll get his email address and he'll know you really want me to meet him."

Hopefully their response will be, "Oh, okay, that's a good idea." You might find this part of the conversation a little difficult, but they won't. The payback is worth it because the introduction will start to move the ball forward. It doesn't mean you don't call people and "use my name" if that's the only option open to you. It's just better to get an introduction.

The Introductory Email

Introducing two people by email is very different from doing it in person. If you're at an event and you introduce a friend to someone he doesn't know, all you need to provide is their names and maybe one sentence about each other (typically what they do or where they work). The two people who have been introduced are under a sort of social obligation to talk. At this point, your job is to be interesting and engaging if you want to talk to this person (and polite and deferential if you find the two of you have absolutely no reason to be talking with each other).

An introduction by email is different. People's inboxes are so overstuffed that you end up competing with their work. Given their ability to prioritize, work will come first. However, if they recognize the email address of their friend introducing you, at some point they will take time out to read it.

At that point, the introductory email may age in the in-box for a while or get acted upon quickly. It is typically just a matter of how pressed for time the individual is and not a reflection on the introduction (or their willingness to get back to you). Here are some ideas for helping your friend make the email introduction.

1. Remind them:
+ What you've done together in the past.
+ How long you've known each other.
+ How you originally met.

2. Position your career history:
+ Achievements when you worked together.
+ Earlier achievements and honors.
+ Later achievements and awards.

3. Encouragement to connect:
+ How you might help the recipient.
+ Why together you will have a great conversation.

In fact, if you really want to help your friend out, send a paragraph or two to be used in the introduction. In that way, your message gets sent the way you would like it repeated and your friend doesn't have to do as much work.

Sample Introductory Email

Denae,

I included my previous note below as a bit of a reminder of the last conversation (so I'm not redundant). First, let me thank you for the invitation to listen to Pam this morning. I really enjoyed her presentation and would like to contact her to see if we could meet sometime. According to what I propose in my book, the best way for this to happen is for you to make an introduction. If you want, you can use the following paragraph:

Pam, I'd like to introduce you to John Davies. He was on the call Monday morning and very much enjoyed your presentation. John has just completed a book entitled *The $100,000+ Career: The Power of Networking for*

Executive Job Change. He asked me if
I could introduce the two of you so you
might get in touch and share your
thoughts about networking. You can
reach John at lawof100@gmail.com.

In the meantime, Denae, let me know if
there's anyone in the networking group I can
help. I hope all's going well. I look forward to
the next time I bump into you at a networking
event.
Sincerely,
John

*Denae took the paragraph I sent her as a
foundation to add her own notes and it made
her task easier.*

The introductory email has one simple goal—to
connect you with an introduction to another person.
With that goal in mind, it's better to keep it short
and to the point. Most important, by helping your
friend write part of the email, you've saved them
time and put yourself in the best light.

How Can I Help You?

And now it's time for the most important question in the entire conversation: Is there anything I can do to help you?

"I mean, this networking thing really works, but this guy says you have to keep doing it when you're employed. It doesn't even have to be for work. It can be for hobbies and all sorts of things. So, is there anyone I can introduce you to?"

This is the crux of networking. By helping others, you expand your network and build stronger connections that can last a lifetime.

To achieve these types of connections, it's important to help others feel comfortable enough to make requests of you. It helps build relationships and helps you start the flow of networking rather than making your conversation a one-time event.

Building out your network gives people the opportunity to contribute and get involved in your life, and it gives you a chance to offer your support to others.

By using the techniques in this chapter, you can stop putting off those calls to people who really want to help you and start getting introductions from them. A majority of the people you know really do want to help—they just don't know how. Now that you've given them a way to help by providing an introduction, you've also brought them closer to you. The people in your network no longer function as individuals, but as a team with one goal in mind. They will conspire to help you get a really great job. They are your support system. The next chapter is all about how you manage your job search conspiracy.

CREATING CO-CONSPIRATORS

"'It's dead straight. Just don't be short.'"

"There was this awful hush all of a sudden. You could feel a clamminess come over the group. I'd broken a monster caddy rule: Never speak in the negative tense."

—*Who's Your Caddy?*, by Rick Reilly

A S YOU BUILD UP your networking relationships, it's important to surround yourself with people who can function as your support system when times get tough. It's also good to have them around to celebrate when things go well, although it's usually a lot easier to find people who want to join a party than to do hard work.

There are different types of people who can help you create this support system, but the important thing is that they have the right characteristics. A golfing trip I took to Ireland is a good illustration of what you want (and what you don't want) for your support system.

I love to play golf and I have been fortunate enough to play a lot of great courses. Whenever possible, I like to walk, but many courses in the U.S. insist on using carts. One of the best experiences I've had was flying out with a group of friends and playing ten courses in Ireland in eight days. With minor exceptions, there wasn't a cart to be seen. This meant we had caddies for every round.

For a couple of the rounds I got paired with my great friend Kevin Hart. Kevin's a white-haired bear of a man with a great sense of humor, which we needed when we met our caddies at one of the oldest golf courses in Ireland: Lahinch.

It appeared Kevin's caddy stepped out of the pub (after an all-nighter) and onto the course at eight in the morning. Through the rest of the day, it wasn't clear if he'd ever seen a golf course, and Kevin told him he'd give him a bigger tip if he'd just leave. Unfortunately, either through a misguided sense of dignity or a desire to really irritate the American, his caddy lasted the entire eighteen holes.

I drew a young, silent man who appeared to have course knowledge—he just didn't feel it was important to share it. The fourth hole at Lahinch is a par-five designed by Old Tom Morris. It's a short hole at four hundred seventy yards, but when you tee off you have no idea where the green is located. The second shot is blind as well, and you have to hit over a large dune toward the green.

I was hitting the ball well but I missed my drive short and to the left. Standing in the fairway, I couldn't wrap my head around the idea of hitting a three-wood straight at this big hill, which is what my caddy was telling me to do. I kept asking him for reassurance and he looked exasperated, telling me to just drive it straight at the hill and stop worrying about it. I hit a perfect shot right where he told me to. "Take that, Tom Morris!" I beamed as I handed him the club.

"You're fooked," he replied. "You'll be right in a sand trap. It'll be hard to make par from there"

"What are you talking about? I hit it right where you told me to."

"I know," he replied. "I just didn't expect you to hit a good shot."

It was downhill after that. I could never tell if his advice was straight or if he was compensating for something he wasn't telling me as he handed me a club. Kevin and I walked the rest of the round wishing a rabid goat would attack our caddies.

Co-Conspirators Are Like Good Caddies

That's an example of what to avoid when you're building your support system. A good caddy knows that you never put a negative thought into the mind of a golfer. Telling a player "don't hit it short" right before he or she putts can be disastrous. It introduces a bad thought into the golfer's head that wasn't there before. It takes away confidence. It's not unlike the experiment where you stand on the corner of a busy street and just look directly up in the sky when there's nothing actually there. Eventually, a group of people will congregate around you to look up into the sky. Even though they can't see anything up there, it's hard to resist the suggestion of other people staring up in the sky.

Earlier in our trip, Kevin and I played at Old Head and had great caddies. Old Head is actually a new course and one of the most spectacular places to play golf in the world. Situated on a finger of land that juts into the ocean, most of the holes are bordered on one side by a steepness that runs straight to the waves crashing against the rocky cliff.

Our caddies were in their early twenties—one a semiprofessional boxer and the other the son of the pro at a nearby course. They had a great sense of humor, telling us jokes and keeping everything light even as we donated another ball to the fish.

At most links courses, if you're not in the fairway and your name isn't Tiger Woods, you'll have a challenging time making par. At 325 yards from the green, my ball peaked through the rough on a par-five. "Take a six-iron," my caddy told me.

"But I'll never even get close with that," I complained.

"You just need to get it back out onto the fairway," he replied, in his lilting Irish accent. "Once we do that, you've got a nice easy shot onto the green." I swung hard through the foot-high fescue and moved the ball about a hundred yards forward. I was starting to think that playing on a course like this wasn't going to be very much fun when my caddy took my club and said, "That's what I like to see." My next shot sailed right next to the green.

Throughout the rest of the day, it was my caddy and me versus Old Head. When I hit a great shot, he led the cheer. When I duffed a long iron, he focused me on what to do next, not what had just happened. He'd tell a joke to break the tension before a short putt to win a hole. He started betting with Kevin's caddy on how we would do against each other.

The rest of the day went much like that and it was the best scoring round of my trip. Our caddies were a mix of cheerleader, psychologist, mad shot-creating scientist, and stand-up comic. They told us more funny stories that day than I'd heard in a week at my home course. Everyone had a great time and by the end of the round, we were the big-tipping Americans.

"Psssst! Let me tell you something. Just between you and me."

The caddies had done something that most people never think about. They had done something very powerful, and yet very easy to do. They made us feel like insiders. Between their mix of local history and humor, they made us co-conspirators.

"Co-Conspirator" is the title I use on my Law of 100 business cards. Co-conspirators are what you create when you call people to ask for introductions to new people and it's what you hope to create when you meet those new people and start building stronger relationships.

What to Do When People Ask "What Number Are You On?"

You'll know when you start creating co-conspirators. As you talk with people, you'll notice them starting to ask strange questions.

"What number are you on?" was the first question that took me by surprise. I hadn't really thought about precisely quantifying whether people should count either as a "new" contact or as the result of an introduction. But I started keeping track so I could give people an answer. "Thirty-seven," I would say, and it made the game of giving and getting introductions a lot more fun. The questions can also start getting more elaborate.

"If I introduce you to my brother in Texas, what number will he be? I mean, does it count if you call him instead of meeting him face-to-face?"

"If I introduce you to someone who doesn't end up meeting you, does it count?"

"If I introduce you to three people, does that count as one or three?"

When you start getting questions like these, you'll start realizing that you've created a group of co-conspirators. This is extremely important because now they're not just people who take your phone call—they are advocates who have signed up to help you find your next great opportunity!

The most important reason to create co-conspirators is to make the search process fun. As you continue calling people, the process becomes more like a game and less like work. When they hear how enthusiastic you are, they become enthusiastic as well. When they see that there's something they can really do right now to help you out (when all they have to do is introduce you to someone new), they feel as good about themselves as they feel about helping you.

Your Personal Advisory Board

As you build up your network, you will intuitively start sorting your contacts into different groupings. Newer contacts are those you may want to move higher up the relationship pyramid. Other contacts may be people who won't become close personal friends but who you may be able to help in the future.

You don't have to sort your contacts into rigid categories. As you progress through your career, your relationship with the people in your network will change. They might move or switch industries. The scope of your job may require more diverse contacts for information and advice.

While creating your merry band of co-conspirators, there will be some who have a bigger role than others. One category you do want to have some of your contacts sorted into is what Terry Goldfarb-Lee calls the "invisible" Personal Advisory Board.

The Personal Advisory Board isn't like a corporate board of directors. There are no minutes by the corporate secretary or yearly meetings to fly off to. In fact, the members of this board might not even know they're on it.

The Personal Advisory Board consists of a group of people who act as your trusted advisors. These are the people you call when you are introduced to new opportunities that you might not be sure about. They can function as a sounding board as to whether you truly are a good fit for an organization that is interested in you. They can help you assess whether you need to change direction or open yourself up to a new set of targets. They can be your caddy.

Your Personal Advisory Board should consist of approximately eight to ten people, although there's no magic to that number and in practice you should follow the dictum "the more, the merrier." Terry suggests that two-thirds of your board should consist of service providers, primarily because they have the largest network of connections that can help you. When I wrote this book, I lived in Orange County, California. It seemed like there was only one degree separating me and anyone I wanted to meet. Your Personal Advisory Board is that one-degree conduit to the people you may want to meet or whom you may want to know more about.

As I knew fewer service providers (and hadn't reached a Level Five relationship with many of them), my board wasn't stacked in their favor. I created my board much like a corporate board—selecting people for specific skills or connections that might help me in my search.

Members of your Personal Advisory Board can assist in several ways:

+ Provide information about your target opportunities.
+ Warm up any target or prospect before you make your call.
+ Review your approach before a call.

+ Hold you accountable to your weekly or biweekly progress.

I didn't tell all the members of my board that this was their role, but in my mind I knew why each of them had been added. They would provide me with support at critical points during my search.

In order to make the most of your board, you need to be specific about how they can help you. You need to make it very clear what you would like them to do for you. Remember that they are helping you, and—to paraphrase another Tom Cruise line from *Jerry Maguire*—you need to help them help you.

For example, if you're asking them to make a specific introduction for you, you need to give them (preferably in writing) a set of tools such as the following:

+ The goal of the introduction.
+ What you would like them to say (with specific phrases about how to describe you).
+ Measurement of success (how will they know they've done a good job for you).

If you don't give your board guidance as to how you want them to help you, they'll do what they're comfortable with and that is not always what's right for your search.

Other Stakeholders in the Business of You

In addition to your Personal Advisory Board, there's a larger group of co-conspirators that could also be referred to as stakeholders. These are people who you have either already asked for introductions, may have known for a long time, or people you've met along the way who are interested in helping you.

Give a Quick Update

It is also important to keep this group informed as to how your search is progressing. Every six weeks, you should send an email that acts like a pop-up screen. You can give them a short status as to how your search is going—and always include a phrase such as "no need to reply, but I'm still available" so they don't feel as if they need to break the rhythm of their day to reply to your email.

One-to-Many Reminders

While it's important to keep in touch with everyone you meet through your networking efforts, the time required can feel overwhelming. One of the benefits of continuing to participate in networking meetings (even after you've landed), is that you can reconnect with up to thirty people at one time. These are the golden days of fishing with dynamite.

The Quick Survey

One of the best ways in which your co-conspirator network can help you is by participating in a quick survey. The quick survey is an email blast with a very specific goal. For example, you might have discovered a new company that might be a great opportunity for you to investigate. You can send out an email to your co-conspirators and discover if anyone has any connections at that company.

The quick email blast serves a couple of purposes. You potentially gain insight and information about the company you're targeting. In addition, though, you're demonstrating your initiative and the approach that you're taking in performing your search. This helps people understand the way you'll approach your next opportunity and, for many in your network, you'll reinforce their comfort in helping you.

You should treat the people you meet during your search like precious gems. By thinking about them as your co-conspirators, you will all be united by a common goal. Some of your contacts will play a larger role in helping you find your next great job than others. All of them, however, will remember being a part of your search. And in the future, you can be *their* caddy, you can be *their* co-conspirator.

CHAPTER 10

TOOLS OF THE TRADE

"The people are insane.
They just like talking to salesmen."

—John Williamson to Shelley "the Machine" Levine,
explaining why he won't get paid his commission
in the movie *Glengarry Glen Ross*

M Y WIFE WAS SHELL-SHOCKED for days after watching *Glengarry Glen Ross*. She thinks sales is all about what happens to the Jonathan Pryce character—that the pressure and stress of being sold to cannot be avoided. It's easy to understand how this happens.

For most people, the two biggest purchases will be a car and a house. The difficulty in buying a new car, for example, is that you only do this every few years. But the person selling to you does this every day—they are practicing and perfecting how to sell you a car.

The big problem with the car sales experience is that there is limited accountability. In today's market, once the salesman sells you the car, there's a good chance you may never see him again. On the other hand, my mother bought new cars from the same person for decades. They lived in the same small town, and if he treated his customers poorly, his dealership would go out of business. Instead, he practiced and perfected how to keep people coming back.

The reason this is important is that you are also now in sales. Your new job when you're in transition is selling the greatest product in the world—you. In order to do this effectively, you need to have a strategy for how to approach the sale and you need some basic tools.

Search Strategies

There are lots of books describing sales strategy in your local library and it can be helpful to leaf through a few of them to get some basic ideas about the sales process. But the most important thing to remember is that your number one strategy for selling the GPW (greatest product in the world) is to build up a network that will take you well beyond your initial sale (i.e., your next position in a company).

Your sales strategy (or job hunt strategy) encompasses more than I address in this book. The strategy addressed here is how to get introduced to the one hundred people who will help you achieve your goal. When I was first in transition, I had a strategy and it seemed sound (at least at the time)—I would meet venture capitalists and one of them would perceive all of my great gifts and hire me to run a company. I didn't say it was a great strategy, but at least it was a strategy.

Metrics for Success

The part I was missing was whether there was any way to measure how I was doing. That's when I sat down with Paul Larson, a coach with Right Management. I told him about the Law of 100 and he had an answer immediately as to what the ratio should be: 50/5. Fifty calls a week and five face-to-face meetings.

Fifty calls every week. That means fifty connections or fifty conversations. Leaving a message on an answering machine doesn't count. Talking with someone's administrative assistant doesn't count (unless their assistant can specifically help your search).

Fifty calls every week. I could do five face-to-face meetings with my eyes closed. Coffee breaks and lunches—I could schedule those. But fifty calls a week. Not calls to your friends just to shoot the breeze, but fifty calls to get an introduction or to follow-up with someone.

Fifty calls every week. I'll confess—I never reached that number. For a couple of weeks I was a danger to all around me as I dialed various numbers while making left turns to get to the five meetings. I decided to sacrifice a few calls for the safety of everyone else on the road.

Fifty calls a week. It's an Olympian metric. While I never achieved it, I still used it because it gave me a big goal to shoot for and it made me dial those extra numbers at the end of the day.

You might want to settle on a slightly different metric—fifty calls or emails a week. You will be able to keep focused on your goal. Emails may seem like cheating, but to get to some of the people you need to reach, it's the only way to initially get through to them. In order to keep focused on the calls, the rule should be to write emails during the hours when you can't call people (usually at night or in the early morning). And an email is only "complete" when you get a response (i.e., a conversation).

Dealing with Rejection

There is one other part about becoming a new salesperson—even if it is for the greatest product in the world. You need to be prepared to deal with a lot of rejection. Calls not returned, emails not answered.

For you, the future of the GPW hangs in the balance. But for them, they're concerned about their own GPW getting her work done, getting home to see the family, getting out to play a round of golf, or advancing the GPW to the next level within their organization.

In order to put the feelings of rejection in context, each day you should call a mix of people you know and don't know. Keep a few of your advisors as rewards or safe havens.

The biggest frustration will not really be rejection. The biggest frustration is inaction—just not being able to get through. Once you get someone on the line and start explaining the Law of 100 (in other words, creating a new co-conspirator), you'll find you'll have a lot of great conversations.

The great fun about the Law of 100 (and I've heard this from dozens of people) is that it makes it a lot easier to talk on the phone because you have a topic that both people find to be interesting. It's not all about you or the person you're talking to—it's about the network that includes both of you.

Obviously, your search strategy is about more than making phone calls and getting introductions. It's about where you're going with your career and your life. But to get to your goal, the Law of 100 will really help. To make the Law of 100 effective, the following sections present some tools that will make it easier for you to reach your goals.

Building the Database

As you went through chapter 2, you started building spreadsheets based on advice from Terry Goldfarb-Lee. And since you did that, you've started calling people and getting introductions. Hey, this is fun. But where's that napkin I wrote Jane's brother's name on?

Now that you've got a large list of people, you need to keep it somewhere—you need a database. This can simply be a spreadsheet (like the call sheet described later in this chapter) or you can buy a sales contact database application like Act! or Goldmine. Another good option, and probably the most widely used, is Microsoft Outlook.

In addition to capturing all the addresses and phone numbers of the people in your network, these programs will save all your outgoing and incoming emails—which is important when you're trying to remember whether you followed up on that introduction or not.

But don't get too hung up about this. It doesn't really matter what technology you use. Before the Fischer Space Pen, astronauts used pencils. An "urban legend" contends that the U.S. government spent billions to develop a pen that could write in a weightless environment. This simply isn't true . All astronauts (Russians *and* Americans) used pencils until Paul C. Fisher undertook on his own initiative to invent the space pen. While it makes a better story when you can talk about wasteful government spending to outdo the Russians, the real moral of this story is that keeping it simple can still be very effective.

For all that it matters, you can keep your contact names and addresses on a piece of ledger paper if that makes you more comfortable—it just gets a little unwieldy as it grows. I only mention this because I have watched executives who still have their assistants print out their emails (although I suspect that this will go the way of the urban legend before too long).

As you build up your database, include everyone you meet. Remember the advice from chapter 2; don't prejudge.

The Phone Is Your Friend

The inspiration for this book came when I realized how much more fun I had making calls to create my "conspiracy of 100" than I did trying to find a job. I've never really enjoyed talking on the phone all that much. But by turning it more into a game, and giving people a way where they could help, it certainly became easier.

I came to realize a number of simple things, things that I probably knew but had never thought much about. For example, calls are better than emails for scheduling, but emails are better than calls for making introductions (because you can address the email to everyone involved, including administrative assistants).

Besides returning calls, the best reasons to use the phone are:

+ Trying to get new introductions from the people you know.
+ Following up calls or sharing information—remember that you're not a vulture preying on new leads, you are building a network.
+ Thanking people.
+ Coaching your referrals—letting them know that someone will be calling them and that you would like them to talk about some specific achievements.
+ Getting a quick response.

The phone is a great tool because it saves time and is very convenient. It's also very efficient. While using a phone takes less time than writing a letter, for most people it shows that you have initiative. It also lets you use notes (or a script), which is extremely helpful to get the most out of your call.

But the phone can also be frustrating. It can seem impersonal and the burden is on you to convey your message clearly. Luckily, the Law of 100 got you an introduction for the call and so he or she is predisposed to want to talk with you. But putting off phone calls is easier than skipping a meeting and that is probably the biggest danger of using the phone.

Be Prepared

Using the phone is like being a Boy Scout: you are successful if you follow the motto "Be Prepared." In addition to the information on the Active Call Sheet (described later in this chapter), you should have immediate access to any reference material that you might need during the call (your calendar, a summary of their business, etc.).

The major purpose of preplanning is to eliminate wasted time; yours certainly, but more important, the time of the person you are calling. A well-prepared phone call sounds focused and professional.

In addition to having the purpose and the best-case end result in mind, you should also consider what you can offer in return—what you can give to help this person more than they'll be helping you.

Earlier, you learned how to make calls to get an introduction as well as how to direct your friends to write the email introduction. The goal of your calls now is either to follow-up from a previous meeting or to schedule your first meeting with someone. If you're scheduling your first meeting, ask for thirty minutes. If it goes well, they'll give you more. Remember, at this point you are just starting to build a relationship.

All of the conventional wisdom recommends that you stand when you're talking on the phone (it apparently helps you to project better). I haven't done this much because I like to write a lot of notes, but many salespeople tell me that it works. I do know that you should definitely smile when you're talking (and that goes for whether you're on the phone or not).

As we all know, there are good times to talk on the phone and bad times. The lesson here is to think about being on the other end of the line when you're making a call. For example, when are good times to call? Seven-thirty is not too early in the morning and five o'clock is not too late at night. In fact, a late-afternoon call can find your contacts stuck in traffic and predisposed to talking with you.

When you get them on the phone, always ask if they have time and if this is a good time to talk. And to make it easier for them when you're trying to schedule a lunch or coffee, give the person a choice of two dates or days.

Phone Call Scorecard

Elle Oliver is an enthusiastic coach at Lee Hecht Harrison's Los Angeles office. She suggests that when you're done with a call, rate yourself. Consciously ask yourself, "How did it go? What worked and what seemed to fall flat?"

By keeping track of this, you can begin to see if you notice any trends. Think about this as if you were participating in the phone call Olympics. Here are some prospective categories for achieving your perfect ten. You can view each of these in terms of "Did Okay," "Need Practice," or "Not Relevant." Here are Elle's criteria for your "dive" into phone calls.

✚ Prepared a script in advance (particularly useful for informational interviews).

+ Had clear objectives for call.
+ Got gatekeeper's name (first and last).
+ Sensed target's verbal style.
+ Adapted to target's style.
+ Introduced self gracefully.
+ Mentioned referral source gracefully.
+ Got to the point quickly.
+ Stated objective of call.
+ Revealed job change positively.
+ Avoided being interviewed by phone.
+ Avoided mailing resume.
+ Suggested time/dates for appointment.
+ Negotiated creatively on roadblocks.
+ Got desired appointment.
+ Repeated time and date.
+ Clarified address, floor, room number, etc.
+ Offered phone number in case of change.
+ Made immediate notes of appointment.

In giving yourself a "grade" on each call, you'll make yourself more conscientious about what you're doing. The reason that you're doing this is not about scoring perfect tens. It should be about putting yourself in the position of the person you are calling and trying to understand how you sound to them.

And always send a thank-you note.

Category	Did OK	Need Practice	Not Relevant
Prepared a script in advance (particularly useful for informational interviews)			
Had clear objectives for call			
Got gatekeeper's name (first and last)			
Sensed target's verbal style			
Adapted to target's style			
Introduced self gracefully			
Mentioned referral source gracefully			
Got to the point quickly			
Stated objective of call			
Revealed job change positively			
Avoided being interviewed by phone			
Avoided mailing resume			
Suggested time/dates for appointment			
Negotiated creatively on roadblocks			
Got desired appointment			
Repeated time and date			
Clarified address, floor, room no., etc.			
Offered phone number in case of change			
Made immediate notes of appointment			

The Active Call Sheet

The primary tool you need for calling "the 100" is a spreadsheet to plan and track the calls you make. Before the start of each week you should have a list of contacts to attempt to call during the week. For a lot of people, fifty may be an unreasonable number (although it's still a good goal). Whatever your target number is, make sure your list contains more than that because you won't reach everyone that week.

Every week you need to look at this list sometime between Friday night and Monday morning. Why? Because Monday through Friday you're too busy calling and meeting people to keep thinking up new names for the week.

The following is a sample of the Active Call Sheet. This is just a foundation and there are some options listed later for you to consider if you want to customize it for your personal use. You may even choose to add a little fuchsia in one of the columns—go wild!

I reserve the first column to track the kind of contact the person represents. I used an "E" or "T" an indicator as to whether the person is employed or in transition. The only reason I recorded this was to make sure I didn't spend all my time talking with fellow job seekers. I wanted to focus my efforts on talking with people who would help me meet my one

	A	B	C	D	E	F
				sample Workbook.xls		
1	Key	Contact	Numbers	Conversation	Date	Result?
2		Vance Caesar	email	set up lunch?		
3	e	Peter Horvath	(555) 555-5555	Great conversation, he'll be out here last week in June	6-Aug	Message
4		Alex Zelikovsky	(555) 555-5555	New consulting assignment, game comes out soon	6-Aug	Message
5		Scott Sheetz	(555) 555-5555		6-Aug	Complete
6		Tim Vaio	(555) 555-5555	Timogen catch-up, Giants dates are 8/31-9/5 or week of 9/20	6-Aug	Message
7	e	Simon Arkell	(555) 555-5555	Grammercy Venture Advisors (knows Steve Oliff)	6-Aug	Message
8		Cap Zublin	(555) 555-5555	Call to set up new lunch and discuss book	23-Aug	Lunch
9	e	Keith Dierkx	(555) 555-5555	Provided me with several companies to meet.		
10	e	John Fontanella	(555) 555-5555	What's your news?		
11		Fred Montoya	(555) 555-5555	See email exchange		
12	e	Roy Scruggs	(555) 555-5555	see email exchange		
13	e	Vinay Asgekar	(555) 555-5555			
14	e	Mike DiPietro	(555) 555-5555			
15	e	Bruce Richardson	(555) 555-5555	How are the new digs? Does this mean I'll never see you in Orange County again?		
16	e	Frank Orchard	(555) 555-5555	Keeping in touch	6-Aug	Complete
17		Andy Berry	(555) 555-5555	Follow-up on Law of 100 and maybe get together for coffee		
18		Karen Myers	(555) 555-5555	Former Usi, email from Kevin Hart		
19		Jerry Farrow	(555) 555-5555	Get together for lunch some time to discuss book		
20		Melanie Offenloch	email	Send both Christmas CDs		
21		Jennifer vanBuskirk	(555) 555-5555	Have you talked with Robert?		
22	u	Dave Quimby	(555) 555-5555	Set up coffee		
23		Don Hicks	(555) 555-5555	See email		
24	e	Jean-Louis Malinge	(555) 555-5555	See print out		
25	e	KrisAasted	(555) 555-5555	Racommended by Fred Thiel, does retained search in the storage industry		
26		Kevin Wagner	(555) 555-5555	How is his business going? Product Marketing.		
27		Mark Thacker	(555) 555-5555	Gitter is going to give me email about him, he runs something at the Tech:Center		

hundred or people who could provide information I needed.

The second and third columns are the person's name and phone number. If they have multiple phone numbers, list them all. This sheet becomes your portable database so you don't need to turn on your computer when you want to make a call.

The fourth column is the most important column on this sheet. This is where you write the first sentence you are going to say to this person when they pick up the phone to answer your call. It's important to get the conversation started on the right foot by knowing what you're going to say when you reach this contact. This is especially important because for any given week your list will contain fifty to seventy-five contact names and it is very difficult to remember what you wanted to say to each of them.

For some contacts, you may also include a goal in this column. For example, there may be a specific piece of information you're interested in (Do you know so-and-so? or Do you know anyone at Company A?).

The fifth column is where you enter the date when the call was completed so that you can track how many calls you complete each week. The final column can be used to describe the result of the call. I use the following words to describe the results:

Complete   I had a conversation and got a result. It may not have been the result I wanted, but I got one. I usually changed the font of this to bold and also changed the color to blue (hey, it's a big win).

Message   I left a message on an answering machine. I often colored this red because I still had to follow up again.

Callback   The person told me they were going to call me back as this was not a good time to talk.

> **Sent** Obviously, this is used to indicate an email. These would stay red until I got a reply, at which point they would change to "Complete" and become another blue win.

You should also keep a couple of other lists. The Follow-up Call List is identical to the Active Call List with the difference that you're using this to schedule a call for next week or some other time in the future. This is either at the request of your contact ("Can you call me back next week?") or as a follow-up to see if they did what they said they would (e.g., talk with their supervisor about getting you an informational interview).

The other list is the "archive." At the end of each week, sort the calls and cut the completed calls from the Active sheet and paste them into the Archive sheet.

Once a week, you should print out all the sheets from the workbook. The archive should give you a history and a bunch of numbers of more frequently called people whom it might be important to call again when you're driving around.

The Active Call List is your plan for the upcoming week. Combined with your calendar (which should have at least five meetings on it—and some would say that at least two of those should be informational interviews), these are the two most important tools at your disposal for proactively building out your network.

Tracking the Number

There are two types of metrics you want to track as you pursue the Law of 100. The first are the cold hard facts of how well you did the past week. You can chart out how many calls and emails have a blue "complete" next to them and then add them up and compare that to your target (did Paul really say fifty?).

You can also add the numbers in a different way to see if you're spending too much time with other folks in transition or if you're focusing on your broader network. These numbers are your report card and your job is to keep them at a steady level.

The other measurement is much more fun. It's the "what number are you on" metric. When you complete a call to someone you recently met (but called for the first time) or to someone where your first contact is a call (preferably based on someone's introduction), list them under the heading "Candidates."

You can then keep another list for the count. These are people you feel are part of your List of 100. Each week, candidates may get moved onto the List of 100. This isn't an exact science as to who got moved from "candidate" to "count," as it should depend as much on gut instincts you've developed as an executive as it does on their responses. It's a matter of being intellectually honest with yourself as to whether you made a connection or not.

For example, if I meet someone who was the CIO for a major corporation and we go have a cup of coffee and there's not really anyone that person knows or is willing to go out of his way to introduce me to, and we don't seem to have anything in common to talk about, I didn't add him to my List of 100.

There are also "raw" new people who I have not necessarily developed any connection with and so aren't ready to be put on the List of 100. On the other hand, I met a lot of people who I still play golf with or meet for a cup of coffee. They may not become Level Five, but I still enjoy their company.

Are You One of My 100?

Here are some things to think about as you create your own set of criteria:

+ Someone who moves the ball forward.
+ Someone comfortable enough with you to introduce you to someone they know well and who they believe may be of help to you.
+ Someone you've had more than one conversation with.
+ Does someone who is not employed count?
+ Is this a major connector to an entirely unknown and untapped network for me?

Now you have the basic tools you need to support your Law of 100 search strategy. Use these to keep motivated and to measure your progress. You can create these tools with a pencil and piece of paper, or you can use your computer to make it easier. As you consider automating these tools, the next chapter will help you understand how you can use technology to support your networking efforts.

USING TECHNOLOGY TO SUPPORT YOUR NETWORKING

Hours are like diamonds,
don't let them waste
Time waits for no one...

—"Time Waits for No One," M. Jagger/K. Richards

I N OUR INCREASINGLY COMPLEX world, the rapid pace of new technology being introduced can be breathtaking. Just as you start to master email, along comes instant messaging. Just as you finally figure out all the buttons on your handset, you start talking straight into your computer. While the following chapter can't cover all the technologies available to support your networking efforts, there are some that you should consider.

Having started a couple of technology companies, I should probably embrace new technologies more than I do. I am not an early adopter. I will play around with various technologies (probably a lot more than the average fifty-year-old and a lot less than the average twenty-year-old). But it needs to be easy and I need to see the value quickly. Most important, I need it to save time.

Technology should be viewed by how much more efficient it makes you, rather than how new or newsworthy it is. From the previous chapters, you can tell what I think are the three most important technologies for executing on the Law of 100:

+ Telephone
+ Email (and contact database)
+ Spreadsheet

Those three tools represent the absolute minimum of what you need to make the Law of 100 work for you. When you evaluate these and other technologies, figure out if they're saving you time or taking more time than they should. And it's not just time spent using them, but also time spent being distracted by them.

In terms of efficiency, you can certainly use your home phone, but then you can only make calls when you're home. With your cell phone, you're connected all the time. This gives you a chance to make calls when there are lulls in your day, as long as they're the right kinds of calls. If you're making a first call to someone or you're calling someone to get an introduction, make sure you have a clear signal as there are few things more annoying than repeating, "Can you hear me now?" This might be a good time to use a landline. But if you're just confirming an appointment with an administrative assistant, your cell phone will work fine.

As far as email goes, if you can afford a device that integrates your phone with a portable email client (like a BlackBerry or Treo device), these can be very useful for leveraging your time more effectively. Whether you're waiting in line to check in at the airport or you're parked and waiting to pick your kids up from school, these devices let you get your work out of the way so you can spend your available time more productively.

Managing Contacts

Many people combine the functions of email, a contact manager, and their calendar in a single program—the most common of which is Microsoft's Outlook. If your background is sales, you might prefer sales force automation tools such as ACT! or Goldmine. While these are good tools, most global

2000 corporations have standardized on Microsoft's Office Suite; which, if you use it, can make your transition to a new company that much easier.

I received a number of the following tips and strategies from J. Lee Braly—an energetic woman and program manager extraordinaire I met at one of the seminars I taught while writing this book. She shares the following, which can be applied to any of these contact management or productivity programs. This is not meant to be all-inclusive, but rather just to give you a few interesting tips and ideas.

According to Lee, the first step is to make sure that you create a contact for every person you want to track. Then, if you're using Outlook, you can click on the "Activities" tab for a contact and see every email that you've sent to or received from that individual—as long as the email is still in Outlook (meaning you haven't deleted it).

Lee suggests using folders to organize and store emails in much the same way she uses physical folders to store physical documents. While I used to do that (and it is effective to a point), I now keep one big folder of email that I call "Archive" as an off-line file in Outlook. I store all my sent email as well as pertinent (i.e., not spam) email I receive here.

Partly this is because disk space is inexpensive and it guarantees I keep most of my email. But it also makes it very convenient for either Outlook or a desktop search tool (more about this in a little bit) to find my history of emailing a specific person.

In addition to listing all your email correspondence with an individual under the activities tab, you can also associate any other Outlook item with an individual. These include tasks, notes, and calendar entries. At the bottom left of each of these forms, there is a button labeled "Contacts."

[Contacts...] [   ]

If you click on that button, a list of your contacts will be displayed. Select one of your contacts to associate with a task or appointment. For example, you might have a lunch appointment with Tom, who got introduced to you by Mike. While Mike won't be joining you for lunch, you can still associate him with the appointment and it will come up when you click on the Activities tab for Mike's contact information (as well as when you look at the Activities associated with Tom).

Another way to use this feature is with email. Perhaps you get an email from Steve Howard that gives you some information about Lee Braly. The Activities tab for Steve will show the email, but you won't see it when you look at Lee because she was not copied on the email. In this case, you can open the email and at the top menu select "View" and then select "Options." The window that opens has a button for "Contacts" that works like the one described above. When you try to close the email, Outlook asks if you want to save it. Select "Yes" and the next time you go to the "Activities" tab for Lee, that email will show up in the list.

In the same way that you can assign one or more contacts to an item, you can also assign it to one or more categories. The reason to do this is to get to quick lists of people who will help you with a specific topic or to identify individuals you want on a specific mailing list. This button is on the right side of various forms, opposite the "Contacts" button.

Categories...	

You can assign one or more categories to each of your contacts. Probably the best illustration of how this is useful is to consider holiday greeting cards. The category of "Greeting cards" might work well because you send them to people who are categorized as "Friends and Family" as well as people in other categories, such as "Suppliers" or "Customers."

Obviously, just like using folders to organize information, categories can multiply and get out of hand. The trick is to really think through how you want to organize your contacts and then resist the impulse to constantly create new categories.

Thanks again, Lee, for those useful tips. There are a number of other courses and books to help you leverage technology, and the best place to start looking for them is at your local library. This lets you review them without investing in books that can be expensive and may not give you any new insights.

Search Technologies

A search can be thought of in two different ways. First is your *outbound ability* to search for information, people, and companies that you're interested in. But it can also be thought of in terms of the *inbound capabilities* of making yourself findable when others are searching.

Your outbound ability to search for information is continuing to change and become more sophisticated at a rapid pace. Probably the best way to keep track is to sign up for an email newsletter from a magazine that covers this technology, such as *e-week*, *PC Week*, or *Information Week*. Two of the more recent developments are proving to be very helpful for busy executives—desktop search and search "bots."

For people like me who have little memory, it seems that each piece of data *in* knocks another, older piece of data *out*. The reason this happens is not because we're all losing our minds. Rather, it's because we're getting pummeled with information in quantities that no one has had to deal with before. To help solve this problem, companies such as Google, Yahoo!, and Microsoft have introduced free desktop search programs.

Basically, these programs index every word in every file on your computer's hard disk. When you bring up the search page, you can enter a few words and—voila—lists of emails, documents, and contact information are presented back to you in as little as a few seconds.

Here's an example. Gary Augusta runs a very interesting group called OCTANe, which has been created to bring more entrepreneurial business to Orange County, California. He asked me if I knew anyone who had created a health care vertical practice in a software company. As it often happens, a few years earlier I met someone who fit that description but she had gone off to start up her own marketing company. I couldn't remember hers or the new company's name, but I typed in "health care, vertical practice" and a few other words and the search returned a number of emails and articles. Within the first few entries I found a record of our last conversation as well as the contact information to forward to Gary. My memory alone would never have been able to help.

Making "You" Show Up in a Search

Making yourself *findable* in a search is even more important than being able to search for others. One way you can do this is by creating a personal Web page. While most people aren't professional Web designers, there are a number of options that can help almost anyone build a website that looks professional and appealing. Whether it's Yahoo!, MSN, 1&1, or any of the other Web-hosting companies, you can find quick, easy, and powerful do-it-yourself solutions.

Most of these sites allow you to use templates to create your own Web pages, add content, graphics, and a personal logo. You can even add video clips if that makes sense for your personal site. Just remember that you're building this site to get your next leadership position and you can build a different site to entertain your friends and family.

Yahoo!, as an example, offers a free tool called SiteBuilder (www.yahoo.com). Yahoo's SiteBuilder templates follow good Web page design principles, which make you look professional in the presentation of your personal brand. What's important is to be able to leave the design of your site to the professionals while you focus on the most important aspect of your site—the content.

In that regard, it's important that you create a compelling home page that clearly communicates who you are and your best attributes. As discussed in the chapter on creating your personal brand, this can be one of the most difficult exercises you undertake in your transition. On the other hand, it can be the most rewarding and will surely help you stand out in a crowd.

You only need a few pages to clearly communicate your message. However, if you've written articles, received awards, or created something innovative in your industry, this is a perfect place to feature links or pages that highlight your accomplishments.

On the other hand, if you want to demonstrate knowledge of an industry you want to transition into, you can create a resource center that lists helpful links to websites and articles about the industry you're targeting. The best advice is to try to remember all the ways you developed your business in your last position and think about how those things fit into your current transition plan. Often, people forget how they created tools for their former employer's business and don't apply the same approach to the business of you!

Blogging

By the time you read this book, writing a blog may be a fad that has passed its time—although the Internet seems to be a perfect medium for self-expression. Regardless of how specific technology progresses, the act of writing a blog (commonly referred to as blogging) is a great way to work on your writing skills. And the winners in the executive suite are usually those who can communicate clearly and effectively. When you surf the Web, you'll see that the most popular blogs are well written—even those that have a less formal style.

Don't let the written word scare you. No matter what your age, you can always improve your writing skills. Get friends and associates to read what you write and offer suggestions. If you're still uncertain, you could take a class or read one of my favorite books of all time, *The Elements of Style*, by Strunk and White.

Maintaining a blog doesn't require that you write every day. What a blog does allow you to do is create a much richer profile of yourself by providing greater detail as to your experience and your philosophy about the role you are looking for.

Building a blog can create additional visibility for you on the Web and can add to your credibility from potential employers. Publishing a blog puts your ideas, approaches, and capabilities in terms of creating solutions out in the public domain. That shows confidence, but it also provides you a location to direct prospective employers or networking contacts where they can learn more about you at their leisure (freeing up their time by making it more convenient to learn about you when they have the time).

There is one potential downside to all of this. Much like the senior picture in your high school yearbook, you may live with the contents of your blog forever. For example, try www.waybackmachine.org. You might find some humorous versions of early websites of former employers before they fully understood how to effectively use the Internet. In the future, you might find your old blog. But if you take it seriously when you're writing it, you should be proud of it when you find it years later.

Social Networking Software

Some of you might be wondering if you can just use social networking sites to meet your one hundred. A couple of years ago, venture capitalists started looking for new things to invest in. Community building or social networking software (anything from Friendster to eHarmony to business software such as LinkedIn and Spoke) seemed to fit the bill. The "social" applications that focused on marketplace activities, such as business development, dating, and building communities where participants can share similar interests seemed to be doing well.

The jury is still out for social networking tools. For example, they seem to offer little value for interactions with people whom you already have relationships with. To keep in touch with them, it is far more efficient to simply send an email or give them a call if you want to ask them a question. You don't need to arbitrarily put a piece of software between you and your friend.

The providers of social networking tools originally claimed that their value lies in helping you locate, establish relationships with, and interact with people you do not already have relationships with. The problem is that this is an attempt to automate something which should be a very human interaction: the introduction. In other words, the social networking software looks to take the social out of the network.

Social networking software typically allows you to use various search criteria to find either a specific individual or individuals at a specific company. You can then see how many degrees separate you from this person (let's say his name is Tom). At this point you can send a pre-scripted email (with a little personalization from you) to the next degree who is someone you know (who we'll call Cathy). Cathy then forwards this introduction to her friend Harry, who then forwards this introduction to Tom.

Does this really sound effective? Without an explicit introduction from a friend, Tom doesn't really know anything about you and it's difficult to figure out why he would care that you're a friend-of-a-friend and being introduced to him.

You can easily contrast this approach to the Law of 100, where Tiffany introduces you to Jay and you begin to establish a relationship with Jay where you developed trust in each other and look for ways to help each other. At some point, Jay becomes comfortable enough to introduce you to Tom (probably sooner than you think if you're sincere in your networking). At that point, Tom will likely help you if he can and you've also tapped into Jay's extended network.

Social networking software shares a number of similarities with software created to automate tasks and contact management for a sales force. Unfortunately, salespeople typically do not want to share their full list of contacts because their Rolodex is what they perceive as their career security.

Social networking software has suffered from a similar problem. Many of the sites list the contact information for every venture capitalist who ever invested in them, but it's impossible to find more than a couple of CEOs of *Fortune* 1000 companies. As a humorous aside, I know a cofounder of a social networking software company that lets his friends log in under his account because they don't want their name in the register.

There has been a shift in focus for some of these companies. LinkedIn has evolved to be a site for job postings that you can then search for people you might know who could sponsor you at a target company. You may also choose to use it as a way to reconnect with people you've lost touch with as you search for them in the LinkedIn network. This isn't exactly nirvana, but it's a lot closer to being a useful tool, especially if there's a specific company that you're interested in and are looking for some background information or an introduction.

My advice is that if you start to use LinkedIn (or another tool), it's better to think of it in terms of looking for "people" to talk to about an industry or a set of companies, rather than looking for openings in a specific company. You still want to establish relationships so that eventually these new friends are comfortable in helping you meet other people.

In review, the most effective tools available today are your office applications (email, word processing, spreadsheet, etc.), the Internet search engines (Google, Yahoo!, etc.), and your personal promotion tools (your personal website, your blog—whatever you use to brand yourself and make yourself findable on the Web).

As far as where all this convergence might get to someday, here's my Orwellian/utopian prediction (you can decide). With the convergence of VoIP (voice-over Internet protocol), every call you make will become a digitized file somewhere on the Web (hopefully in a secure place). Every email you send is also somewhere out there in the Web, along with all of your work on your computer. Almost everything you do for work (and a lot of things you do for fun) is sitting somewhere on the Web

Now just think about the ability to search this worldwide network of information and employ personal analytical tools. You could create huge maps of how you relate to everyone else in the world and how they relate to you. As with all technologies, this can result in good or bad outcomes. Focusing on promoting your personal brand and maintaining your integrity—either in person or on the Web—will help make sure the technology is serving your best interests.

No matter how future technologies evolve, your strongest and most valuable relationships will still be with the people you personally know the best or to whom you've been introduced who are beginning to know you better.

CHAPTER 12

IF ALL ELSE FAILS

"If a man does not make new acquaintances as he advances through life, he will soon find himself alone. A man should keep his friendships in constant repair."

—Samuel Johnson

YOU MIGHT BE THINKING, *The Law of 100 sounds interesting, but what if it doesn't work for me?* This is the point where you have to believe in yourself and give it a try (and continue to be persistent). The Law of 100—the technique of introduction-based networking—is one of the few job search strategies that *you* control. As you take control of your search, here are some final pieces of advice that may help you along the way.

Moving the Ball Forward

While I was writing this book, I talked to recruiters from retained search firms about how much time to spend on presenting yourself to them. Off the record, they confided that most of their clients had no interest in looking at someone who wasn't currently employed. In some strange twist of logic, the qualified person in transition is less attractive than the incompetent working for their competitor.

I went on to ask about how often they checked the database when searching for a candidate. That's a tougher bet than winning the lottery without buying a ticket—their clients give them target companies and that's who they go after.

So how do you beat the odds? You already know that replying to advertisements is a low-margin proposition. And the Internet is a lot better for sports scores than finding the job you really want.

The answer is to keep networking! Be persistent. Pick up the phone and make another call. Go meet someone for another cup of coffee. Go to that networking mixer tonight. Get another introduction.

If there was a way around all of this, it would have been discovered long ago. Your job is to be in the right place at the right time. Getting introduced to new people increases the number of places and times that people can meet you and get to know you.

Remembering the Strength of Weak Ties

Duncan Watts's book *Six Degrees* presents a comprehensive overview of network theory and how things are connected. In discussing the work of sociologist Mark Granovetter, he notes:

> [There is a]…correlation between weak ties and an individual's prospects of getting a job. Job hunting, it turns out, is not just a matter of having a friend to get you in the door—precisely what sort of friend they are is of great importance.
>
> Paradoxically, however, it is not your close friends who are of most use to you. Because they know many of the same people you do and may often be exposed to similar information, they are rarely the ones who can help you leap into a new environment, no matter how much they want to. Instead it tends to be casual acquaintances who are the useful ones because they can

give you information you would never otherwise have received.

Other studies have shown that using strategic connections has a higher probability of paying off for you because fewer people use informal approaches. In the same way that networking provides better opportunities in the long run, the competition also becomes less intense because you're already known by the people who are evaluating you.

Many positions never reach the stage of being advertised, made known to agencies or recruiters, or even listed with human resources. Networking discussions are the only way to learn of these situations.

Create Your Habits

Looking for a great job is not easy. If it were, you wouldn't be reading this book. For the entirety of this book so far, I've avoided the most difficult part of the job search. Getting rejected. Ditched. Dusted. Ignored.

When this happens, you have to constantly beware of getting depressed or dejected. Just when you want to scream "Don't they see this is my life they're playing with?" pick up the phone and make another call! Kiss more frogs. Even salespeople don't like "dialing for dollars," but the phone won't make calls by itself.

When the world seems like it's completely crashing down around you, take a break. Treat yourself to something—maybe just some time in a quiet place or a trip to a noisy Starbucks to people watch. Buy yourself a gift or go for a run.

Then get back to work. Create a habit of networking and do it every day.

Being There

There are very few rules for what you do when you meet someone you've been introduced to. Being yourself is a good idea, because you might end up making a great new friend.

Having good posture is smart, too. I know this sounds like your mom's advice, but you're judged by people before you even open your mouth. You can stack the deck in your favor, though, by being presentable, showing up a little early for appointments, and acting like you belong.

This last one can be tough. I remember my brother Evan taking me shopping in Chicago for my first expensive suit. I walked around with my hands behind my back and acted like a teenager on a first date. My brother set me straight at dinner that night. "John, don't forget, you're the one who's in control. You're the one who has the money."

The light bulb went on. You don't necessarily have to be over-the-top like Donald Trump (pointing to the person you're with and exclaiming that they're the greatest living example of a human being to walk the earth…next to you), but if you find a situation where you really want to work, you need to act like you belong there.

An extreme example of this is a movie based on the novel *Being There*, by Jerzy Kosinski. In Peter Sellers's last movie, he plays Chance, the gardener—a middle-aged man with the mind of an innocent child. Through an improbable set of circumstances, Chance ends up offering advice to the president of the United States. And because he has on a handsome suit, maintains good posture, listens more than he talks, and is *introduced* by a wealthy advisor to the president, he's perceived as a sage.

PRESIDENT: Do you agree with Ben, Mr. Gardiner? Or do you think we can stimulate growth through temporary incentives?

CHANCE:	As long as the roots are not severed, all is well and all will be well in the garden.
PRESIDENT:	…In the garden?
CHANCE:	That is correct. In a garden, growth has its season. There is spring and summer, but there is also fall and winter. And then spring and summer again…
PRESIDENT:	…Spring and summer… (confused)…yes, I see…fall and winter. [smiles at Chance] Yes, indeed.
RAND:	I think what my most insightful friend is building up to, Mr. President, is that we welcome the inevitable seasons of nature, yet we are upset by the seasons of our economy.
CHANCE:	Yes. That is correct. There will be growth in the spring.
PRESIDENT:	…Well, Mr. Gardiner, I must admit, that is one of the most refreshing and optimistic statements I've heard in a very, very long time.

While this makes for great satire, Chance isn't trying to deceive the president—he's just being himself. This does illustrate, though, that people can be predisposed to "hearing" you more favorably as the result of an introduction and some basic work on your part.

Much like the title of the movie, a lot of times success comes along just by being there. When I was first in transition, I went to as many events as possible where I would meet people involved in the world of venture capital. At three different meetings, I exchanged business cards with the same guy, Gary Augusta. After the third meeting, he called me up and wanted to meet. He figured if we were going to be at all the same events that he should probably know me. Now we get together on a regular basis, talk about deals (and the Red Sox), and who we can introduce to each other.

Another benefit of being there is that you'll figure out which networking meetings aren't worth your time in the future. If you don't show up, you'll never know.

Finally, as you start to meet people, you'll want to keep in touch. By continuing to attend networking meetings, you can reach thirty people at a time. This is a very efficient way to stay in touch. Because you're looking them in the eye, this is better than making a phone call.

One on One

Getting together with people is what networking is all about. You won't be asking for a job 99.999 percent of the time. Instead, you'll be asking for information, insight, and advice. You don't want to lose sight of your goal (getting the job you really want), but that can't be the first topic in every conversation.

Before every meeting, place the "just to make sure" call. Make sure the appointment is still on. Make sure it's still convenient. Make sure you don't show up as a surprise.

When you're arranging to meet someone, remind them that you were introduced because they might have some ideas that could help you (and that this is not a job interview). For you, this is an opportunity to get feedback and suggestions about your search. For them, you need to think about how you might help or who you could introduce to them.

Because your getting together is less formal and is more relaxed, it will be more productive. If in the unlikely event the person knows of a position (either within their organization or in another company), they may feel comfortable enough to mention it to you. Even if no position is open (or is about to become open, or is capable of being created), you will still obtain valuable information and referrals to other people.

On occasion, when silences become too long, you might want to steer the conversation toward the worst companies they have heard about. This can be effective because those companies usually make for interesting stories (or good gossip) and they are also the companies that need the most help.

Conversation is truly an art form and we've all met someone we think of as an artist. But for the rest of us mere humans, the rules for conversation (and therefore the rules for networking) are simple. Avoid superficiality. Be genuine, honest, and forthcoming. A great conversation is about "keeping it real." And as I mentioned before, it's also about knowing when to shut up.

Keep Telling Stories

There are some very important things, though, that you want to bring with you to every conversation and every meeting. They are things that only you can bring. They are your stories.

Children and adults and even my pet tortoise like to listen to stories. The elevator pitch describing you during your search or describing your business after you've landed is a creatively told short story. In addition to the pitch (the short story that is you and might also describe where you want to be), you should always have a few other stories on hand to liven up a conversation or create a picture of the type of person you are. Some of these stories are:

+ Job hunting stories—everyone's had good and bad experiences here, but try not to focus too much on this one, unless it illustrates an important point you want to make (maybe about your persistence or resourcefulness).

+ "Against all odds" accomplishment stories—this speaks to your character and accomplishments while you illustrate what you were up against.

+ Personal stories that help to illustrate your point— which is why I've had so much fun writing this book. All the stories in here first came alive in one conversation or another.

Stories are also great for social or business networking events. When someone asks what's new, it's better to have something to say besides, "Nothing much. What's new with you?" A good story, short and to the point, is easier for people to remember and will make it even easier for them to remember you.

While I was developing some of the ideas for this book, I heard from Susan Eskin about a slightly different angle in regards to storytelling. Now that Susan is retired from the software business, she can admit to things like this. At one point, Susan told me that getting an introduction is one thing. But when you make that first contact with the target (she was, after all, in sales), the approach must be artful...a perfect blend of respect, confidence, humor, attitude, and gratitude. Her art was name-dropping: "So subtle that they don't know whether you even realize that you name-dropped! I used to do this with Bruce's name all the time!"

At times, Susan would use this technique with people she didn't really know quite as well as you might have thought. My advice is that if you use someone's name and they don't really know you that well, it'll probably blow up in your face. However, I do know Bruce Richardson (whose name Susan would drop). Bruce has a quick wit and you can read his opinions in the *Wall Street Journal* or in his weekly "alert" for AMR Research (Caution: shameless plug for a company I really love working at). I have also used Bruce's name more often than I should probably admit, but pointing out who your friends are (dropping names) is sometimes the easiest way to move the conversation forward.

The best conversation, though, is when you're talking about how you can help people get what they want. Remember that and people will always want to talk to you because you're the guy who can help and not the guy who needs help.

Write

Another good topic for conversation is to write. At least that seems to have worked for me. In fact, if everyone who's confided in me that they want to write a book actually did write a book...well, maybe you should draw your own conclusions about that.

While writing this, I was living in Southern California. I often told people that I was writing a book about networking. When someone tells me in response that they also like to write, I am always interested in finding out what they write about. If you have any inclination to write, do it.

Writing an article or a white paper can position you as an expert on a specific topic. It doesn't matter if your article was actually published or not, what matters is that you wrote it and it reflects some of your skills and your expertise. A well written white paper can emphasize your potential contribution to an organization. It will provide even more value to the reader if it's a topic they're interested in, so pick your topic in terms of what you love to do or what people are in need of most.

Writing articles or white papers can have a couple of other effects as well. First, it will force you to articulate your knowledge in a way you may not have done before. Capturing your particular expertise on paper will help you polish your thoughts and make you a better conversationalist when describing your ideas or experience.

The second potential consequence is that writing articles can become a means of meeting people with whom you have had difficulty trying to schedule an appointment. I got brushed aside a couple of times by people who didn't see how they could help me. As I persisted, I would mention the book I was working on and that one of the reasons I wanted to meet them was to validate some of the ideas in my book. Under those circumstances, they usually found a way to fit me into their schedule.

My only advice for anyone who takes this tack (interviewing someone for an article as a means to meet them) is to honestly be working on an article or a white paper. Disingenuousness is never a good networking tactic.

Read a Lot of Books (and Give Them Away)

Today's workplace is changing so rapidly that those not able to pick up new ideas and run with them will be passed by. Employers are desperately looking for people who are flexible, open to new concepts, and adaptable to new management strategies, new technologies, and new procedures.

How can you fit that profile? Read a book a week. Know what the pundits are saying. You don't have to agree with them but you can help the person you're talking with by being able to clarify both sides of an argument. For example—what's the real impact of outsourcing? Do you understand the changes that are going on by off-shoring work in a global economy? How is this good for America, and what are the risks? You don't have to be an expert, but by demonstrating that you are a student of our changing world, you become more valuable to those around you.

You should also read broadly. The Internet makes it easy to find obscure books and articles—

especially when you're thinking of changing industries. Search the niche publications for trends and new technologies.

Finally, buy someone a book today. If you have a great conversation with them about a topic you've read a great book about, buy them a copy and send it to them. Include a note telling them why you thought they might like this book.

Don't do this if you think the gift might make them feel uncomfortable. For example, if this is after an interview instead of a conversation with someone you're networking with, you don't want to make it appear that you're trying to bribe them. In that case, find some reviews on the Internet or an article by the author and send that via email instead.

Books help extend our conversations and create a common understanding or perspective. In our fast-paced society, though, it's often difficult to find out about great books that don't make the bestseller list. Help people find these gems and they will remember your help for a long time.

Keep the Network Alive

Building a network to search for a job is hard work. It takes time to get to know people and to establish new relationships. When you're trying to establish a network while also trying to figure out where the money is going to come from, it can be frustrating.

But once you've got your new position, you need to continue to add new contacts to your database—forever! This is probably not the last time you're going to be involved in a job search and you won't want to go through this exercise again from scratch.

You need these people—only now you don't need them quite as immediately. When you get that new position, update everyone so they know where to find you and so they can tell you how to find them when they move. Send personal notes to recruiters because now is when they (and more important, their clients) will be interested in you.

Building out your contact list should be based on people you can help and those who can help you in return. One way to keep your list alive is to send out holiday cards or emails.

In December a lot of holiday cards and emails cross our desks. You may want to consider picking a different day (maybe International Talk Like a Pirate Day or Arbor Day) to do an email blast to reach out. If this becomes a tradition and you send your current information and any interesting news, people will remember you (because, let's face it, do you even know when Arbor Day is?).

It's also good to review articles in the media (especially for your industry or geography). When you see an article about a contact or her company (or about something you know might interest her) drop a note with the article as an attachment.

Networking never stops. Those who maintain and grow their networks locate new positions 50 percent faster than those who must rebuild them once they are in a search. Your network becomes even stronger when people in your network know one another and do business with each other.

Networking is an active behavior. It's about being an explorer, continuing to learn, and finding new possibilities.

At its heart, networking is about the desire to serve and contribute to others. It becomes a lifestyle choice. It has nothing to do with quid pro quo, tit for tat, or any other formal exchange. Networking is about giving, volunteering, and being helpful.

And, most important for you as you continue your search, networking is about persistence. A persistence best described by the thirtieth president of the United States, Calvin Coolidge.

Nothing in the world can take the place of
persistence.
Talent will not do it.
Nothing is more common
Than an unsuccessful man with talent.
Genius will not.
Unrewarded genius is almost a proverb.
Education will not.
The world is full of educated derelicts.
Persistence and determination alone are
omnipotent.
The slogan "Press on" has solved and always
will solve
The problems of the human race.

So press on! Keep your network alive, you'll be
amazed at who you meet and who you can help.

EPILOGUE

NETWORKING LED TO MY current role at AMR Research, where we provide the global business community with "research and advice that matters." Informally, though, we also offer an opportunity for senior executives to network, through our conferences as well as through introductions where we believe our clients may benefit from working together.

Interestingly, networking also led to a job I didn't enjoy at all. At other times, it helped land consulting work and speaking engagements. Networking doesn't have an end point. It needs to be part of an ongoing process of career development. Building out a personal and professional network requires an investment of the most precious capital you have—your time. But the return on that investment will not only be progressively better roles, but a more satisfying career.

While I wrote this book, I got emails from people testifying to the power of introduction-based networking. I set up calls with them to hear what their number was—the number of new people to whom they were introduced. I wanted to hear their stories. I wanted to get a better understanding of how this process worked. What they told me mirrored my own experiences.

They told me that it isn't just a matter of finding the right people. It is about having a series of dialogues that push you harder to think about what you truly want and what unique insights and experiences you have to offer. For the people who actively used the Law of 100, there was no single conversation that led to a job. Rather, an aggregation of conversations leads to a tipping point. For many, this point was the job offer.

But the tipping point can also be a fresh insight into what is most important to you. Talking with new people pushes you to be more articulate about what you want and how you describe your passions and interests. The Law of 100 provides you with a process to have more of these conversations in a concentrated period of time.

Success with the Law of 100 isn't merely measured by the salary you're offered. Your metric is the network you build. That network will continue to teach you about the market and yourself. While the world of work changes at a rapid pace, the network you establish will keep you current. By taking a structured approach to introduction-based networking, you'll stay relevant and connected for the rest of your career.

ACKNOWLEDGMENTS

THERE ARE FAR TOO MANY people to thank for their help while I developed the ideas presented here and set them down in this book. While standing at the chasm of offending by omission, I'll take the risk and thank the following people who provided assistance, guidance, inspiration, and other forms of support.

At Sourcebooks, Peter Lynch has provided invaluable editorial advice and guidance.

William Brown, my agent at the Waterside Literary Agency, helped me understand what it meant to write a book proposal, but even more important, he gave me early support that the book I'd written would be valuable to other people in transition.

There are a lot of other people I talked with, presented to, bought coffee for, had lunch with, and helped build out my network while I was writing this book. Listing the entire network would be fairly dull, but the following people provided me with ideas and support while I wrote this book.

Jim Armstrong, Anette Asher, Helen Atkinson, Gary Augusta, Mark Aument, Marc Averitt, Al Barna, Michael Bellomo, Luis Berga, Andy Berry, Jack Bicer, David Black, Lee Braly, Terry Bruggeman, Steve Burgess, Denae Butte, Vance Caesar, Tom Cheung, Karis and Jim Chodzko, Erika Conboy, Pat and Karen Courts, Kevin Covert, Dave Cox, Carla Cushman, McKenzie, Evelyn, Cody, Keegan, Caitlin, Scott, and Sue Davies, Scott DeFord, Keith Dierkx, Matt Elson, Susan Eskin, Phil and Kathleen Everson, Jerry Farrow, Tom Fedro, Jim Ferguson, Dan Fesman, Randy Finchum, Dan Fischer, Lawrence Flon, William Frawley, Xuan French, Mark Friedman, Tony Friscia, Kimberly and Jay Fulcher, Mary Galvin, Ray Garcia, Dave Gaylord, Wens Gerdyman, Robert Gifford, Eric Gilbert, David Gitter, Ed Glassmeyer, Terry Goldfarb-Lee, Gene and Hannah Golub, Dave Grant, Bart Greenberg, Sara and Tom Griffen, Rich Guha, Patrick Hansen, Lisa Hanson, Kevin and Gina Hart, Rich Hayden, Mark and Renee Hein, Gary Hessenauer, Rodney Hexter, Don Hicks, Don Holbrook, Eric Holmberg, Peter Horvath, Jay

Houlihan, Steve Howard, Charlie Hughes, Robert Humphrey, Glen Kacher, Michelle Kalnas, Ken Kaufman, John Kelly, Toni Khan, Zain Khan, Mike Kilgore, Kimberly Knickle, Jennifer Laser, Dave Lemme, Andrew Lesko, Mitchell Levy, Jane Macfarlane, Carleen MacKay, Lisa Malkki, Mike Marks, Gregg Marston, Ray Martin, Rod McDermot, Roger B. McNamee, Scott McNealy, Mike and Judy McNulty, Dan Mees, Carrie Messer, Stephanie Miles, Fred Montoya, Brian Morrow, Mariel Mulet, Scott Mumby, John Murray, Paul Niven, Randy Noe, Ryan Northington, Hope and Sue O'Donnell, Elle Oliver, Michael Busby Oliver, Bonnie Olson, Nina and Bhavesh Patel, Jeff Patterson, Jim Pelusi, Greg Petrisor, Dave Piersma, Dave Quimby, M. R. Rangaswami, Scott Raskin, Toby Redshaw, Brad Remillard, Phil Ressler, Bruce Richardson, Katrina Roche, Tom Roche, Brian Rochlin, Emily G. Rodriguez, Dale Rogers, Chris Roon, Carol Ross-Joynt, Murray Rudin, Laura Ruffing, Jeff Sakaguchi, Tony Salerno, Darius Sankey, Nevin Sanli, Chikara Sano, Peter Santora, Dave Santore, Joseph V. Santoro Jr., Mohanbir Sawhney, Jim Schoessling, Danny Schunk, Roy Scruggs, Scott Sheetz, Ed Shi, Steve Shipley, Stephen M. Shore, Ryan Shuck, Dave Simbari, Steve

Sipe, Rich Skvarna, Ken and Tina Slosberg, Rick Smith, Jim Smith, Peter Sobiloff, Peter Sola, Cruce Stark, Steve Martin, Bryan Stolle, Nan Stothard, Jerry Sullivan, Craig Sundheimer, Fred Thiel, John Tomko, Marshall Toplansky, Nancy Troutman, Brian Turchin, Tim Vaio, Derek, Ellen, Owen and Grace van Bever, Jennifer van Buskirk, Luis Villalobos, Tom Wadsworth, Peter Waller, Frank Wanderski, Carl Wellenstein, Peter Weller, Peter West, Cathy and Andy White, Chris Wong, Geza X, Scott Zahn, Alex Zelikovsky, Michael Zigman, Rick Zipf, and Casper W. Zublin Jr.

RECOMMENDED READING

THE FOLLOWING ARE JUST a few of the books that will provide you with deeper background in terms of some of the concepts described in *The $100,000+ Career.*

Books to Start a Conversation

Thomas L. Friedman, *The World Is Flat: A Brief History of the Twenty-First Century,* 2005.

Roger McNamee, *The New Normal: Great Opportunities in a Time of Great Risk,* 2004.

Thomas W. Malone, *The Future of Work: How the New Order of Business Will Shape Your Organization, Your Management Style, and Your Life,* 2004.

Seth Godin, *All Marketers Are Liars: The Power of Telling Authentic Stories in a Low-Trust World,* 2005.

William Strunk Jr., E.B. White, Roger Angell, *The Elements of Style*, 2000.

Books to Help Your Job Search

Richard Nelson Bolles, *What Color Is Your Parachute?*, 2005.

Carleen MacKay and Brad Taft, *Boom or Bust: Career Management Workbook*, 2004.

Richard J. Leider, David A. Shapiro, *Repacking Your Bags: Lighten Your Load for the Rest of Your Life*, 1995.

Books and Articles about Network Theory and Social Networks

Stanley Milgram, "The Small World Problem," *Psychology Today*, May 1967, pp 60–67.

J. Travers and S. Milgram, "An experimental study of the small world problem," *Sociometry* 32, 425 (1969).

Mark Granovetter, "The strength of weak ties," *The American Journal of Sociology*, Vol. 78, No. 6, May 1973.

Mark Granovetter, *Getting a Job*, 1974, 1995.

D. Watts, S. Strogatz, "Collective dynamics of small-world networks," *Nature*, 393, 1998.

Malcolm Gladwell, *The Tipping Point*, 2000.

Duncan J. Watts, *Six Degrees: The Science of a Connected Age*, 2003.